D0910855

The Bible in Translation

Anne Rice
August 14, 2003
Navarre Beach

Bruce M. Metzger (Ph.D., Princeton University) is George L. Collord Professor of New Testament Language and Literature, Emeritus, at Princeton Theological Seminary and the author or editor of numerous important volumes. A past president of the Society of Biblical Literature and the *Studiorum Novi Testamenti Societas,* he has made valuable contributions to textual criticism, philology, paleography, and Bible translation. He is ordained in the Presbyterian Church (USA) and has served on committees for three major Bible versions, chairing the NRSV translation committee.

cover illustration: *St. Jerome in His Study,* by Albrecht Dürer (1514)

The Bible in Translation

Ancient and English Versions

Bruce M. Metzger

Baker Academic

A Division of Baker Book House Co
Grand Rapids, Michigan 49516

© 2001 by Bruce M. Metzger

Published by Baker Academic
a division of Baker Book House Company
P.O. Box 6287, Grand Rapids, MI 49516-6287

Second printing, January 2002

Printed in the United States of America

Library of Congress Cataloging-in-Publication Data

Metzger, Bruce Manning.
    The Bible in translation : ancient and English versions / Bruce M. Metzger.
        p.   cm.
    Includes bibliographical references and indexes.
    ISBN 0-8010-2282-7 (pbk.)
    1. Bible—Versions—History. 2. Bible. English—Versions—History. I. Title.
BS450 .M46   2001
220.5'09—dc21   2001037427

For information about Baker Academic, visit our web site:
www.bakerbooks.com/academic

Contents

Preface

It is common knowledge that the Bible has been translated into more languages than any other piece of literature. What is not generally appreciated, however, is the great increase in the number of different translations that have been produced relatively recently, that is, during the nineteenth and twentieth centuries. Before this period, the church, it must be confessed, had been rather slow in providing renderings of the Scriptures in other languages.

According to a recent calculation, there are some 6,800 living languages in the world.[1] Estimates of the number vary because judgments differ as to whether a particular form of speech should be called a separate language or even a distinct dialect. In certain instances, local governmental decree has given language status to a dialect. In other instances, what are really distinct languages have been regarded as mere dialects, as is the case of many of the so-called dialects of Chinese. Linguistically, they are quite distinct languages, but because of their orthographic dependence on Mandarin Chinese, they have generally been considered dialects.

Whatever the precise number of languages may be, it is certainly surprising that by the year A.D. 600, the four Gospels had been translated into only a very few languages. These were Latin and Gothic in the West, and Syriac, Coptic, Armenian, Georgian, Ethiopic, and Sogdian in the East—to which also Nubian might need to be added. One might have expected that Augustine and other Christian leaders in North Africa would have provided a transla-

---

1. More exactly, according to Barbara F. Grimes, in 2000 there were 6,809 living languages, distributed as follows: the Americas, 1,013; Africa, 2,058; Europe, 230; Asia, 2,197: the Pacific, 1,311. See *Ethnologue*, vol. 1, 14th ed. (Dallas: SIL International, 2000), p. 846.

tion of the Gospels into Berber or Punic or that Irenaeus and his successors would have made a translation into the Celtic dialect used in Gaul. But there is no evidence of the existence of such versions in antiquity, despite the presence of Christian communities in these areas.

When the art of printing with movable type was invented by Johannes Gutenberg in 1456, only thirty-three languages had any part of the Bible. Even when the Bible society movement began some two centuries ago, only sixty-seven languages had any portions. During the nineteenth century, however, more than four hundred languages received some part of the Scriptures, and within the first half of the twentieth century, this figure increased by more than five hundred. This rapid increase in the preparation of versions of the Bible is due to the role played by Bible societies, Wycliffe Bible Translators, and similar organizations.

The history of the translation of the Bible can be divided into four major periods. The first period includes the efforts to translate the Scriptures into several of the dominant languages of the ancient world. The second important period of Bible translating was related to the Reformation, when renderings were no longer made from the Latin Vulgate translation but from the original Hebrew and Greek text into the vernaculars of Europe. The third period may be called the great missionary endeavor, when pioneer translators undertook the preparation of renderings into hundreds of languages and dialects, in many of which there was previously often not even an alphabet.[2] Such work is still going on, while a fourth period has already begun. This is characterized primarily by translations being produced in newly developing nations, where native speakers often assume primary responsibility, with missionaries sometimes serving as consultants. This has many advantages, since it is invariably easier for properly trained people to translate into their own mother tongue than into a foreign language, and the end product is likely to be more effective.

By the opening of the year 2000, the entire Bible had been made available in 371 languages and dialects, and portions of the Bible in 1,862 other languages and dialects. The following is a summary, by geographical area and type of publication, of the

---

2. For information about alphabets, see Peter T. Daniels and William Bright, eds., *The World's Writing Systems* (New York: Oxford University Press, 1996).

number of different languages and dialects in which the publication of at least one book of the Bible had been registered by the American Bible Society as of January 1, 2000.

Statistical Summary

Continent or Region	Portions	Testaments	Bibles	Total
Africa	218	267	142	627
Asia	228	212	113	553
Australasia/Pacific Islands	172	194	30	396
Europe	106	29	62	197
North & Central America/Caribbean	41	25	7	73
South America/Mexico	135	233	16	384
Constructed Languages	2	0	1	3
Total	902	960	371	2,233

Part 1 of the present book describes all of the ancient versions of which significant portions have survived today. Part 2 discusses a selection of English versions, chosen from the sixty more or less different English translations of the whole Bible and from the further eighty or so of the New Testament alone.

Gratitude is expressed to the faculty of Dallas Theological Seminary for the invitation to deliver the W. H. Griffith-Thomas Lectures during the winter term of 1992. Material in four of the following chapters was published in the quarterly journal *Bibliotheca Sacra* in 1993 and is reproduced here by permission.

Bruce M. Metzger

PART 1
Ancient Versions

one

Ancient Versions of the Old Testament Made for the Use of Jews

The Septuagint

The Septuagint is the traditional term for the Old Greek translation of the Hebrew Scriptures. The word means "seventy" and is often abbreviated by using the Roman numeral LXX, referring (with some rounding off of the figure) to the seventy-two translators reputed to have produced the version in the time of Ptolemy II Philadelphus (285–246 B.C.). The translation is not only the earliest but also one of the most valuable of ancient biblical versions. Whether one considers its general fidelity to the original, its influence over the Jews for whom it was prepared, its relationship to the Greek New Testament, or its place in the Christian church, the Septuagint stands preeminent in the light it casts on the study of the Scriptures.

The story of the origin of the Septuagint is given in a document of uncertain date called the *Letter of Aristeas*.[1] The letter purports to be a contemporary record by a certain Aristeas, an official at the court of Ptolemy Philadelphus, who claims to have personal knowledge as an eyewitness of the following details.

Being of a literary disposition, Ptolemy wished to make a collection of the world's best literature. His librarian, Demetrius of Phalerum, called his attention to the Hebrew Scriptures as being worthy of a place "in your library since the law which they contain . . . is full of wisdom and free from all blemish" (§31). At once the king sent ambassadors to Eleazar, the Jewish high priest at Jerusalem, loading them with gold and jewels and royal salutations (§33), and requested him to send a copy of the Hebrew Scriptures, with learned men who could translate the text into Greek.

From each of the twelve tribes, Eleazar selected six elders who were well versed in the Jewish law (§46) and, with presents for the king, put in their hands a sumptuous copy of the Scriptures written in letters of gold in Jewish characters (§176). Upon their arrival in Alexandria, the seventy-two translators were conducted to a quiet house on the island of Pharos (not mentioned by name) in the harbor of Alexandria, where every provision was made for their needs. So they set to work; as they completed their several tasks, they would reach an agreement on each by comparing versions. Whatever was agreed upon was suitably copied out under the direction of Demetrius (§302). By happy coincidence, the task of translation was completed in seventy-two days (§307). Demetrius then called together a number of the leading Jews of the city and read the translation to them. It was at once approved as an accurate rendering (§310), and a curse was invoked on any who would alter the text by any addition, transposition, or deletion (§311).

The apologetic interest of Aristeas is revealed in a lengthy vindication of the purpose and function of the Jewish law (§§128–71),

---

1. This letter has survived in twenty-three manuscripts, which have been collated by André Pelletier, S. J., for the series Sources chrétiennes (Paris: Editions du Cerf, 1962). The most recent English translation is by R. J. H. Shutt in *The Old Testament Pseudepigrapha*, vol. 2, ed. J. H. Charlesworth (Garden City, N.Y.: Doubleday, 1985), pp. 7–34. For a full discussion of problems connected with the letter, see Moses Hadas, *Aristeas to Philocrates* (*Letter of Aristeas*) (New York: Harper, 1951) and Sidney Jellicoe, *The Septuagint and Modern Study* (Oxford: Oxford University Press, 1968), pp. 29–58.

as well as in a still longer section that describes a banquet and the table talk between Philadelphus and each of the seventy-two translators, designed to exemplify the wisdom, moral insight, intellectual ability, and philosophical acumen of the Jewish people (§§187–300). The writer, however, is aware that he has overdone the encomium on Jewish wisdom, for he adds: "I suppose it will seem incredible to those who read my narrative in the future" (§296).

Most scholars who have analyzed the letter have concluded that the author cannot have been the man he represented himself to be but was a Jew who wrote a fictitious account in order to enhance the importance of the Hebrew Scriptures by suggesting that a pagan king had recognized their significance and therefore arranged for their translation into Greek. The actual motive for undertaking the work, it is now generally agreed, arose from the liturgical and educational needs of the large Jewish community in Alexandria. Many members of this community had forgotten their Hebrew or let it grow rusty and spoke only the common Greek of the Mediterranean world. But they remained Jews and wanted to understand the ancient Scriptures, on which their faith and life depended. This, then, was the real reason for making the Greek Septuagint, the first translation of the Hebrew Scriptures.

From internal considerations, the date of the letter may be assigned to about 150–110 B.C. It was known to Josephus, who paraphrased portions in his *Antiquities of the Jews* (12.12–118). Philo's account of the origin of the Septuagint (*On Moses* 2.25–44) reproduces certain features of Aristeas, but there are also divergences. For example, Aristeas (§302) represents the translators as comparing their work as they wrote it and producing an agreed-on version, whereas according to Philo each of the translators, working under divine inspiration, arrived at identical phraseology as though dictated by an invisible prompter.

In the following centuries, Christian authors further embellished the narrative of Aristeas. According to Justin Martyr at the middle of the second Christian century, the scope of the translators' work embraced not just the Law but the entire Old Testament.[2] Later that century, Irenaeus, bishop of Lyons, stated that Ptolemy, fearing that the Jewish translators might conspire to conceal the truth found in

2. In Justin Martyr's *Dialogue with Trypho* (68.7), the mention of the "translation of the seventy elders" relates not to a Pentateuchal passage but to Isaiah.

their sacred books, put them in separate cubicles and commanded them each to write a translation. They did so, and when their translations were read before the king, they were found to give the same words and the same names from beginning to end, "so that even the pagans who were present recognized that the scriptures had been translated through the inspiration of God."[3]

It is significant that the translators, whether working as a group or as individuals, and in spite of natural tendencies to literalism or to the use of Hebraisms, here and there avoided literalistic renderings of phrases congenial to another age and another language. The Almighty is not called a "Rock"; "Lord" is substituted for the Sacred Name; anthropomorphisms are toned down—God does not repent, is not seen, has not a hand.

Such modifications were not uniformly introduced, but still the changes are too frequent and remarkable to be ascribed merely to chance. A few examples will be sufficient. In Genesis 6:6–7 the statement that God "repented" for having made humankind is softened into the milder expression "He took it to heart." In Exodus 24:9–10 we are told that Moses and Aaron, Nadab and Abihu, and seventy of the elders of Israel went up and saw the God of Israel. In the LXX this becomes "They saw the place where the God of Israel stood." In Joshua 4:24 "the power" is substituted for "the hand" of the Lord; and in Isaiah 6:1, though visual perception of God is allowed to stand, "the train of his robe" is converted into "his glory." In Exodus 15:3 "The Lord is a warrior" becomes "The Lord is one who crushes wars." Changes like these indicate a disinclination to ascribe the human form or human passions to the Divine Being.

Underneath the accretions and behind the story as told by Aristeas, modern scholars are generally in agreement on the following points: (1) The Pentateuch was translated first as a whole, and it has a certain unity of style that distinguishes it from the later translations of the Prophets and the Writings. (2) The homogeneity of the translation makes it improbable that so large a number as seventy were at work on the Pentateuch. (3) The Hebrew scrolls

---

3. Irenaeus, *Against Heresies* 3.21.2 (in Eusebius, *Ecclesiastical History* 5.8.11–15). For an account of still further elaborations in the third and fourth centuries, see Jellicoe, *Septuagint and Modern Study*, pp. 44–47, and Hadas, *Aristeas to Philocrates*, pp. 73–80.

were possibly imported from Palestine. (4) The language of the version is similar to the Greek used in vernacular papyri found in Egypt and contains Egyptian words.[4]

It was a difficult task for the first translators to form and partly invent a vocabulary that would express the content of the Pentateuch. There is no explicit evidence that they possessed either dictionaries or word lists. Thus, when attempting to determine the meaning of a word, they drew upon the context, etymology, and exegetical traditions. For the translation of the later books, translators were sometimes guided by that of the Pentateuch. In spite of these sources of information, sometimes the renderings must be described as guesswork—especially in the case of Hebrew words occurring nowhere else in the Bible.

The various books in the Septuagint vary as to literal and free translation. Examples of free (or even sometime paraphrastic) translations are Job, Proverbs, Isaiah, Daniel, and Esther; literal translations are the books of Judges (the B text), Psalms, Ecclesiastes, Lamentations, Ezra-Nehemiah, and Chronicles.

The Septuagint differs from the Hebrew Scriptures both in the order of the biblical books and in the number of books included. The traditional division into the Law, the Prophets, and the Writings is abandoned, and the books are arranged according to their literary character: (1) Pentateuch and historical books, (2) poetical and sapiential books, (3) prophetical books. Within each group, the sequence does not correspond to that of the Hebrew canon.

Some of the books not included in the Hebrew Scriptures are Greek translations of Hebrew originals (Tobit, 1 Maccabees, and Ecclesiasticus, also known as the Wisdom of Jesus the Son of Sirach); others are of Greek composition (Wisdom of Solomon; 2, 3, and 4 Maccabees; and others).

Apart from possessing additional books, the Septuagint also differs from the Hebrew Bible in the supplemental matter contained in certain books that are common to both. The Greek form of the Book of Esther, which in Hebrew contains 167 verses, has six extra sections, an additional 107 verses. The Book of Daniel receives three supplements; in the English Apocrypha of the King James

4. This suggests that the translators were Alexandrian and not Palestinian Jews.

Version, these are called the History of Susanna, Bel and the Dragon, and the Song of the Three Holy Children.

On the other hand, the Book of Job is about one-sixth shorter
in the Septuagint than in the Hebrew text, and the Book of Jeremiah (besides extensive transposition) lacks about one-eighth of
the material present in the Hebrew text. In both cases, it may well
be that the translators were working with a Hebrew text sharply
different from that which later became the traditional Masoretic
text. The translation of the Book of Daniel was so deficient that it
was wholly rejected by the early Christian church, and a translation made in the second century A.D. by Theodotion was used
from the fourth century onward in its place.

The importance of the Septuagint as a translation is obvious.
Besides being the first translation ever made of the Hebrew Scriptures, it was the medium through which the religious ideas of the
Hebrews were brought to the attention of the world.[5] It was the
Bible of the early Christian church, and when the Bible is quoted
in the New Testament, it is almost always from the Septuagint version. Furthermore, even when not directly quoted in the New Testament, many of the terms used and partly created by the
Septuagint translators became part and parcel of the language of
the New Testament.

By the end of the first century of the Christian era, more and
more Jews ceased using the Septuagint because the early Christians had adopted it as their own translation. At an early stage, the
belief developed that this translation had been divinely inspired,
and hence the way was open for several church fathers to claim
that the Septuagint presented the words of God more accurately
than the Hebrew Bible. The fact that after the first century very,
very few Christians had any knowledge of the Hebrew language
meant that the Septuagint was not only the church's main source
of the Old Testament but was, in fact, its only source.

The earliest copies of the Septuagint, being made by hand,
would soon come to differ among themselves, according to the

5. The first-century A.D. Greek treatise *On the Sublime*, attributed to Longinus,
refers to Genesis 1:3 and 9 as follows: "The lawgiver of the Jews . . . says in the
introduction to his Laws, 'God said'—what?—'Let there be light, and there was;
let there be earth, and there was'" (9.9; trans. J. A. Arieti and J. M. Crossett [New
York: Mellen, 1985], pp. 57f.).

judgment and accuracy of the scribe making them. This danger had been anticipated in the curse invoked in the *Letter of Aristeas* upon anyone who altered the rendering of the Seventy. Eventually, the text became so unreliable that in the third century Origen made a heroic attempt to purify it. His first step was to collect all existing Greek versions of the Old Testament. He then proceeded to transcribe the several versions in parallel columns and to indicate in the column devoted to the Septuagint the relation in which its wording stood to the current Hebrew text. This huge work, called the Hexapla, presented in six narrow columns (1) the Hebrew text; (2) the Hebrew text transliterated into Greek characters (to facilitate the reading of the unvocalized first column); (3) the severely literalistic Greek rendering made about A.D. 140 by a proselyte, Aquila, who attempted to reproduce individual Hebrew words exactly; (4) the Greek rendering of Symmachus (probably later second century), which explained the *content* in a readable style; (5) the Septuagint, which by means of Origen's critical symbols provided detailed information concerning the differences between the Septuagint and the Hebrew text; and (6) a Greek rendering ascribed to Theodotion that has much in common with the Septuagint, so much so that it is often regarded as a free revision rather than an independent rendering. According to Eusebius, Jerome, and other fathers, the last four columns (Aquila, Symmachus, Septuagint, and Theodotion) also existed in a separate form known as the Tetrapla.

The descriptions of the Hexapla given by several church fathers have been confirmed by the discovery of copies of continuous fragments of leaves of the Hexapla. These help us to understand what an enormous task it must have been to arrange the whole Old Testament in a series of codices so gigantic as the Hexapla. Since each horizontal line displayed only one or two Hebrew words, with the corresponding renderings into Greek, it is improbable that any attempt was made to reproduce the Hexapla (or even the Tetrapla) as a whole. The originals, however, were long preserved at Caesarea in Palestine, where they were deposited, perhaps by Origen himself, in the library of Pamphilus. There they were consulted by writers and owners of biblical manuscripts. But in 638 Caesarea fell into the hands of the Saracens, and from that time the library was heard of no more.

Near the beginning of the fourth century, the idea occurred to Pamphilus and his friend Eusebius to publish copies of the fifth column, for they believed that Origen had succeeded in restoring the Old Greek version to its primitive purity. Other Christian recensions of the Greek Old Testament date from the fourth century. These are attributed to Lucian, a presbyter at Antioch, and to Hesychius, an Egyptian bishop martyred in A.D. 312, and were primarily stylistic in character.

Over the centuries, the Septuagint has had a wide influence. It became the basis for daughter versions of the Old Testament in many languages, including Old Latin, Coptic, Gothic, Armenian, Georgian, Ethiopic, Christian Palestinian Aramaic, Syriac (in Paul of Tella's translation around 616 of Origen's Hexaplaric text), Arabic, and Slavonic. Finally, the importance of the Septuagint can be judged from the fact that it remains to this day the authoritative biblical text of the Old Testament for the Greek Orthodox Church.

Eventually, the Septuagint was repudiated and execrated by Talmudic scholars, who declared that the day on which the Law was translated into Greek was as unfortunate for the Jews as that on which the golden calf was made. A fast day was appointed to mark the calamity. Subsequently, manuscript copies of the Septuagint were made only by Christian scribes.[6]

The Jewish Targums

The Targums are interpretive renderings of all the books of the Hebrew Scriptures (with the exception of Ezra, Nehemiah, and Daniel) into Aramaic. Such versions were needed when Hebrew ceased to be the normal medium of communication among Jews. Consequently, it became necessary at the public reading of Scripture in the synagogue to present also an oral translation into the Aramaic vernacular of the populace. For a reading from the Pentateuch, the Aramaic translation followed each verse of the Hebrew; for a reading from the Prophets, three verses were followed by the Aramaic rendering.

At first the oral Targum was a simple paraphrase in Aramaic, but eventually it became more elaborate and incorporated explan-

---

6. For English translations of the Septuagint, see chap. 5, under "Charles Thomson's Bible (1808)."

atory details inserted here and there into the translation of the Hebrew text. The functions of such glosses were various, including (1) to resolve textual difficulties by interpreting obscure words or simplifying syntax, (2) to harmonize conflicting texts, (3) to reconcile the biblical text with accepted tradition, (4) to incorporate specifics of Pharisaic-rabbinic Judaism into the text, (5) to provide specificity to historical, juridical, or religious allusions, and (6) to either strengthen or mitigate the force of a scriptural passage.

For a long time, there was strong prejudice against writing the Targums, and when they did come to be written down, they represented the labors of many minds, even though the actual fixing of the form may have been the work of one individual. Two officially sanctioned Targums, both produced first in Palestine and later revised in Babylonia, are the Targum of Onkelos on the Pentateuch and the Targum of Jonathan on the Prophets, both of which were in use in the third century of the Christian era.

During the same period, the Targum tradition continued to flourish in Palestine. In addition to fragments and citations that have been collected, the Palestinian Targum to the Pentateuch is found, primarily, in three forms. The two that have been the most studied are Targum Pseudo-Jonathan and the Fragmentary Targum, the latter of which contains renderings of only approximately 850 biblical verses, phrases, or words. In the mid–twentieth century, a neglected manuscript in the Vatican library, identified as Neofiti 1, was discovered to be a nearly complete copy of the Palestinian Targum to the Pentateuch. Though copied in the sixteenth century, its text has the distinction of being the earliest form of the Palestinian Targum. It is somewhat less paraphrastic than Pseudo-Jonathan in that its explanatory additions are fewer in number and more terse in expression.

The wide divergences among these Targums clearly indicate that they are "unofficial," in that their text was never fixed. There are no reliable data as to who the authors and compilers were, under what circumstances and for what specific purposes they labored, and how textual transmission was maintained. Biblical texts purposely *not* translated in public include the story of Reuben and Bilhah (Gen. 35:22), the story of Tamar (Gen. 38:13ff.), the account of the golden calf (Deut. 9:12–21), the account of David and Bathsheba (2 Sam. 11:7–17), and the story of Amnon (2 Sam. 13:1ff.), because of their offensive nature, whereas the

Priestly Blessing (Num. 6:24–26) was not translated because of its sacrosanct status.

Although the several Targums display certain common features, there are also many differences of rendering among them, ranging from literalistic to paraphrastic and incorporating a variety of kinds of explanatory comments. Sometimes an anthropomorphic expression in the Hebrew concerning God is softened or eliminated in the Targum. In speaking of the relationship of God to the world, reverence for the God of Israel led the targumist to employ surrogates for the Deity, such as "Word" (*memra*), "Glory" (*yeqara*, *ʿiqar*), or "Presence" (*shekinah, shekinta*). Thus in Genesis 1:16–17 Targum Neofiti 1 reads, "*The Word of the Lord* created the two large luminaries . . . and *the Glory of the Lord* set them in the firmament," and in Genesis 2:2–3 it reads, "On the seventh day *the Word of the Lord* completed the work which he had created . . . and *the Glory of the Lord* blessed the seventh day" (material added by the targumist is in italic).

As was mentioned earlier, besides providing an Aramaic rendering of the Scripture text, the targumist also sometimes provided interpretive expansions. Typical of such interpolations are the following:

> And whatever Adam called a living creature *in the language of the sanctuary,* that was its name. (Targum Neofiti 1, Gen. 2:19)

> *Behold, I have given them the span of* one hundred and twenty years *(in the hope that) perhaps they might repent, but they have not done so.* (Targum Neofiti 1, Gen. 6:3)

> And he [Moses] reached Mount Horeb, *above which the Glory of the Shekinah of the Lord was revealed.* (Targum Neofiti 1, Exod. 3:1)

> May Reuben live *in this world,* and not die *in the second death, in which the wicked die in the world to come.* (Targum Neofiti 1, Deut. 33:6)

An extraordinarily expansive paraphrase occurs in Targum Pseudo-Jonathan at Genesis 4:8, where the Hebrew text fails to tell us what it was that led Cain to murder his brother. The targumist supplies the reason: Cain and Abel had a profound theological argument about the relationship between the divine attributes of mercy and justice.

Cain said to Abel his brother, *"Come, let us both go out into the field."* *And it came to pass, when they had gone out, both of them, into the field, that Cain spoke up and said to Abel, "I perceive that the world has been created through mercy, but it is not governed according to the fruit of good deeds; and there is partiality in judgment. Therefore your offering was accepted with favor, but my offering was not accepted from me with favor."* *Abel answered and said to Cain, "The world was created with mercy, and it is governed according to the fruits of good deeds, and there is no partiality in judgment. It is because the fruit of my deeds was better than yours and more prompt than yours that my offering was accepted from me with favor."* *Cain answered and said to Abel, "There is no judgment, no judge, no other world; there is no fair reward given to the righteous nor punishment exacted from the wicked."* *Abel answered and said to Cain, "There is judgment, there is a judge, and another world; there is fair reward given to the righteous and punishment exacted from the wicked."* *On account of these matters they were quarreling in the open field.* And Cain rose up against Abel his brother, *and drove a stone into his forehead,* and killed him.

Despite their self-professed purpose to be a translation and/or explanatory paraphrase of Scripture, here and there the Targums also present instances of what is termed converse translation,[7] in which the Aramaic text contradicts what is said in the Hebrew. This modification is accomplished through a variety of devices, including the addition or deletion of the negative particle or the replacement of the original biblical verb with another of opposite meaning. Neofiti on Exodus 33:3 reads, "I will not remove *the Glory of my Shekinah* from among you," whereas the Hebrew text reads, "I will not go up among you." Cain's cry in the Hebrew text, "Behold, you have driven me this day from the land, and from your face I shall be hidden" (Gen. 4:14), is changed to read, "Behold, you have driven me this day from upon the land, but *it is not possible for me* to be hidden from you" (Targums Onkelos and Neofiti 1). In both these instances, the targumist was unwilling to accept

---

7. See M. L. Klein, "Converse Translation: A Targumic Technique," *Biblica* 57 (1976): 515–37; and R. P. Gordon, "'Converse Translation' in the Targums and Beyond," *Journal for the Study of the Pseudepigrapha* 19 (April 1999): 3–21.

the implication that God's presence and power could be circum-scribed or limited.

In passing through the territory of the descendants of Esau, the Israelites were instructed in Deuteronomy 2:6, "You shall buy food from them for money, so that you may eat; you shall buy water from them, so that you may drink." Since this verse is followed by the observation that "these forty years the Lord your God has been with you; you have lacked nothing," the buying of food and water appeared to be inappropriate to the targumist. So he contra-dicted the biblical text; Targum Neofiti 1 reads, "You need not buy food from them for money, since manna from heaven descends for you; neither need you buy water from them, since the well of water ascends with you, up to the mountain tops and down into the valleys."

According to biblical law, divorce was permitted and proce-dures were institutionalized (so Deut. 24:1–4; Isa. 50:1; Jer. 3:1). Nevertheless, Malachi declares that "[God] hates divorce" (2:16). Here the targumist directly contradicts the plain meaning of the text and renders it, "For if you hate her, divorce her."[8]

All translations of the Bible are necessarily interpretive to some extent, but the Targums differ in that they are interpretive as a matter of policy and often to an extent that far exceeds the bounds of translation or even paraphrase. It is perhaps against such license that Rabbi Judah (second century A.D.) declared with paradoxical vehemence, "He who translates a biblical verse literally is a liar, but he who elaborates on it is a blasphemer."[9]

---

8. According to Etan Levine, the reason for the targumist's "interpreting the verse contrary to both content and context may be polemical, since early Chris-tianity strongly opposed divorce" (*The Aramaic Version of the Bible* [Berlin: de Gruyter, 1988], p. 151).

9. *Tosephta*, Megillah 4.41, ed. M. S. Zuckermandel (Jerusalem: Bamberger & Wahrmann, 1937), p. 228.

two

—

Ancient Versions Intended Chiefly for Christians

Of the several ancient translations of both Old and New Testaments, the Syriac versions and the Latin versions are generally considered the most important, both for their own sakes and for their having become the bases of many daughter translations. It has been disputed whether the Scriptures were first translated into Syriac or into Latin.

The Syriac Versions

At Antioch of Syria, the third largest city of the Roman Empire, the followers of Jesus were first called Christians (Acts 11:26). Though most of the mixed population of Antioch were acquainted with Greek, when the new faith spread elsewhere in Syria during the second half of the second century, the need was felt for a rendering of the Scriptures into the mother tongue of the populace. This was Syriac, a branch of Aramaic that was akin to Hebrew, though using a different script (called Estrangela; later, other forms were used).

From a very early date, the center of Syriac-speaking Christianity was Edessa (now Urfa in southeast Turkey). The church there, destroyed in 201 during a flood, may be the oldest known Christian edifice. The town soon became the most important bishopric in Syria. Large and well-built villages developed up to the desert edge. The gospel had a great number of devoted followers throughout all that region.

At the close of the second or beginning of the third century, parts of the New Testament began to circulate in Syria in what is called the Old Syriac version. Only two manuscripts of this version, both containing text from the Gospels, have survived. These are known as the Curetonian and the Sinaitic Syriac manuscripts, written in the fifth and fourth centuries respectively.

There was current also at the close of the second century an edition of the four Gospels in one continuous narrative. This had been compiled by Tatian, a native of Assyria who had become a Christian in Rome between 150 and 165, where he was a pupil of Justin Martyr. Whether Tatian's work was first published in Greek at Rome about A.D. 170 or in Syriac in his native land has not been determined with finality. In any case, for the next several centuries Christian congregations throughout the Middle East made use of his harmony, known as the Diatessaron (Greek for "through the Four"). Unfortunately, all of the witnesses to the Diatessaron that are extant today, with the exception of one imperfect leaf of Greek text, are secondary and tertiary witnesses.

The form of the Syriac Bible that came to prevail in Eastern churches has, since the ninth century, been called the Peshitta, meaning "simple" or "common." It is not known whether the term refers to its simple, nonarchaic language or to its unifying of different existing translations.

The origins of the Peshitta Old Testament are shrouded in uncertainty, but in part it would seem to be the work of Jews, and in the Pentateuch, at least, there appear to be tenuous links with the Targums. Those who suppose Christian, or Jewish Christian, origin usually locate the translation in Edessa. On the assumption of

Jewish origin, however, one may think either of Edessa or of Adiabene, the Jewish kingdom east of the Tigris.

The question whether the translators of the Old Testament were Jewish or Christian has been hotly debated, both in antiquity as well as today. Recently, however, it has been suggested that this should not be posed as a question of either/or, since it is quite possible that some books were translated into Syriac by Jews and others by Christians.

It must not be assumed, however, that the Christian translators were of gentile background, but rather that they were converts to Christianity from Judaism. It is generally recognized that a sufficient knowledge of Hebrew among Christians of gentile background would be extremely unlikely. Furthermore, had the incentive to translate a book, or books, of the Old Testament come from gentile Christians, then the translation would have been made from the Septuagint rather than the Hebrew, since the former had rapidly established itself as the authoritative text of the Old Testament for Christians. *common*

The diversity of translators who produced the Peshitta version is reflected in the strikingly diverse style and quality of the rendering. The Pentateuch is very literal, which is true also for the Song of Songs; Psalms and the Minor Prophets are free translations; Ezekiel and Proverbs are close to the Targums; Job is servile and sometimes unintelligible; Ruth is a mere paraphrase. Furthermore, the influence of the Greek Septuagint is obvious from the inclusion of Syriac translations of non-Hebraic books of the Apocrypha in Peshitta manuscripts. The late M. P. Weitzman argued that the Old Testament Peshitta "was put together about 200 C.E. by a small Jewish community estranged from the Rabbinic majority, and the community eventually embraced Christianity, bringing the Old Testament Peshitta with them."[1]

The manuscripts extant today present considerable variety in the number of books and the order in which they are placed. Some manuscripts have, after the Pentateuch, a section comprising the books of Joshua, Judges, Job, Samuel and Kings, Proverbs, Ecclesiasticus, Ecclesiastes, Ruth, and Song of Songs. In other manuscripts, Ruth, Esther, Judith, and Susanna are grouped as

---

1. M. P. Weitzman, *The Syriac Version of the Old Testament: An Introduction* (Cambridge: Cambridge University Press, 1999), p. 1.

the Book of Women. The Psalter is commonly found divided into twenty sections. Several manuscripts also contain a variety of pseudepigraphic works.

As for the New Testament, the process of producing the Peshitta version from the Old Syriac probably began before the end of the fourth century and seems to have been completed no later than the time of Rabbula, bishop of Edessa (A.D. 411–35). Since the Syrian church did not (and does not) accept as canonical the four lesser General Epistles (2 Peter, 2 and 3 John, and Jude) and the Book of Revelation, the Peshitta New Testament contains only twenty-two books. The Peshitta remains the authoritative biblical text of Syriac-speaking churches: Syrian Orthodox, Church of the East (or Chaldean Christians), Syrian Catholics, Malabar (or St. Thomas) Christians, and the Syro-Malankarese Church.

Following the completion of the Peshitta in the fourth or fifth century, two other Syriac versions of the New Testament were made. At the beginning of the sixth century, Philoxenus, the Jacobite bishop of Mabbug (Hierapolis) in eastern Syria, commissioned Polycarp, a chorepiscopus (rural assistant to a bishop), to revise the Peshitta version on the basis of Greek manuscripts. Now, seemingly for the first time in Syriac, to the twenty-two books included in the Peshitta New Testament, the other five books were added. This work was completed in 508. Since the Philoxenian version had been sponsored by Jacobite ecclesiastics, it was used only by the Monophysite branch of Syriac-speaking Christendom.

In the year 616, the Philoxenian version of the New Testament was drastically revised throughout by Thomas of Harkel. He made use of readings derived from Greek manuscripts in the library of the Enaton near Alexandria. The chief characteristic of the Harclean version is its slavish adaptation to the Greek, to such an extent that here and there even clarity is sacrificed. Occasionally, instead of a native Syriac word, the Harclean uses a Greek loanword transliterated into Syriac.

About the same time, Paul, the Jacobite bishop of Tella in Mesopotamia, made a Syriac translation of the Greek text of the Septuagint as contained in the fifth column of Origen's Hexapla (see p. 19 above). Produced with great care and accuracy, it is an important witness to the text of the Old Testament because it preserves

Origen's critical symbols, which have disappeared from nearly all the Greek manuscripts copied from the original Hexapla.

Finally, to round out this account of Syriac versions, reference should be made to yet another Syriac version, more properly designated the Christian Palestinian Aramaic version. The language of this version is the Aramaic dialect used in Palestine during early Christian centuries. Its only claim to be called Syriac rests upon the script in which it is written, which resembles somewhat the Estrangela Syriac script. The language came to be used by Melchite Christians in Palestine and Egypt during the sixth, seventh, and following centuries.

From the foregoing sketch of half a dozen ancient Syriac translations, one can recognize the vitality and scholarship of Syrian church leaders in antiquity. The significance of these Syriac versions can also be appreciated from the circumstance that they became the basis, at least in part, of translations in other languages. The early Armenian rendering of the Gospels, made in the fifth century, shows influence from the Old Syriac text, while the Old Testament, as would be expected, generally follows the Hexaplaric recension of the Septuagint. The Georgian Bible, completed, it seems, by the end of the sixth century, had an Armenian-Syriac foundation. The Peshitta Syriac version was also the basis of the Sogdian and some of the Arabic versions.

The Latin Versions

It would be difficult to overestimate the importance of the influence exerted by the Latin versions of the Bible and particularly by Jerome's Latin Vulgate. Whether one considers the Vulgate from a purely secular point of view, with its pervasive influence on the development of Latin into Romance languages,[2] or whether one has in view only the specifically religious influence, the extent of its penetration into all areas of Western culture is al-

---

2. An example of the influence of the Vulgate on the development of vernacular languages among the Romance peoples is the suppression of everyday derivatives from the common Latin word *verbum*, meaning "word." The forms do indeed occur in the religious, technical sense, meaning "the Word," but in the popular speech of the people, they are replaced by derivatives from the late Latin word *parabola*; for example, French, *parole*; Italian, *parola*; Spanish, *palabra*; Portuguese, *palavra*.

most beyond calculation. The theology and the devotional language typical of the Roman Catholic Church were either created or transmitted by the Vulgate. Both Protestants and Roman Catholics are heirs of terminology that Jerome either coined or baptized with fresh significance—words such as salvation, regeneration, justification, sanctification, propitiation, reconciliation, inspiration, Scripture, sacrament, and many others.

The historian of the Latin versions of the Bible is confronted with difficult and disputed problems, not least of which are the questions when, where, and by whom the earliest Latin rendering was made. Because the language used by the church at Rome was Greek until the mid-third century, the Old Latin versions would not have originated there, but within those early Christian communities that used Latin. Probably by the end of the second century A.D., Old Latin versions of the Scriptures were in circulation in North Africa. In Carthage, Tertullian (ca. 150–ca. 220) and Cyprian (ca. 200–258) quoted long sections of both Testaments in Latin. Since one finds numerous and far-reaching differences between quotations of the same passages, it is obvious that there was no one uniform rendering; some books were apparently translated a number of times, and no single translator worked on all of the books. The Old Testament was not translated from the Hebrew but was based, it appears, on a pre-Hexaplaric form of the Greek Septuagint. In this way, Western churches became familiar with the deuterocanonical books of the Old Testament.

Noteworthy Old Latin readings frequently agree with the Greek text of Codex Bezae and the Old Syriac. On the whole, the African form of the Old Latin presents the larger divergences from the generally received text, and the European the smaller. The diversity among the Old Latin witnesses is probably to be accounted for by the assumption that scribes, instead of copying the manuscripts mechanically, allowed themselves considerable freedom in incorporating their own and others' traditions. In other words, the Old Latin was a living creation, constantly growing.

The roots of the Old Latin versions are doubtless to be found in the practice of the double reading of Holy Scripture during divine services, first in the Greek text and then in the vernacular tongue. In the written form, the translation would at times have been interlinear; later on, manuscripts were prepared with two columns of text, sometimes arranged in shorter or longer lines (called *cola* and *commata*) for ease of phrasing during the public reading of the lessons. The pre-Jerome translations in general lack polish and are often painfully literal. The Gospels stand in the sequence of Matthew, John, Luke, and Mark in the Old Latin manuscripts *a, b, d, e, ff, q, r*. Here and there one finds noteworthy additions to the text. For example, in Matthew 3:16 the Old Latin manuscript *a* states that when Jesus was baptized, "a tremendous light flashed forth from the water,[3] so that all who were present feared." Old Latin manuscripts give various names to the two robbers who were crucified with Jesus,[4] and Mark's account of Jesus' resurrection is expanded in Old Latin manuscript *k* at 16:4 with the following: "But suddenly at the third hour of the day there was darkness over the whole circle of the earth, and angels descended from the heavens, and as he [the Lord] was rising in the glory of the living God, at the same time they ascended with him; and immediately it was light."

By the close of the fourth century, there was such a confusing diversity among Latin manuscripts of the New Testament that Augustine lamented, "Those who translated the Scriptures from Hebrew into Greek can be counted, but the Latin translators are out of all number. For in the early days of the faith, everyone who happened to gain possession of a Greek manuscript [of the New Testament] and thought he had any facility in both languages, however slight that might have been, attempted to make a translation."[5]

As a consequence, there grew up a welter of diverse Latin translations. Among them three types or families of texts gradually developed; Cyprian (d. 258) represents the African text, Irenaeus (ca. 130–ca. 200) of southern Gaul represents the European, and Augustine (d. 430) the Italian. Characteristic of each family are certain renderings; for example, as a translation of the Greek word *phōs* ("light"), the African family prefers *lumen*, the European *lux;*

---

3. Perhaps this is meant to suggest that when "the heavens were opened," God's resplendent light was reflected from the water of the Jordan.

4. For these names, see the chapter "Names for the Nameless in the New Testament" in my *New Testament Studies: Philological, Versional, and Patristic* (Leiden: Brill, 1980), pp. 33–38.

5. Augustine, *On Christian Doctrine* 2.16.

for the Greek *dokimazō*, the African prefers *clarificare*, the European *glorificare*.

In these circumstances, the stage was set for the most decisive series of events in the whole history of the Latin Bible. In the year 383, Pope Damasus urged Jerome (ca. 342–420), the most learned Christian scholar of his day, to produce a uniform and dependable text of the Latin Scriptures; he was not to make a totally new translation but to revise a text of the Bible in use at Rome. Jerome's first inclination was to say "No, thank you" to the pope's invitation. He wrote:

> You urge me to revise the Old Latin version, and, as it were, to sit in judgment on the copies of the Scriptures that are now scattered throughout the world; and, inasmuch as they differ from one another, you would have me decide which of them agree with the original. The labor is one of love, but at the same time it is both perilous and presumptuous—for in judging others I must be content to be judged by all. . . . Is there anyone learned or unlearned, who, when he takes the volume in his hands and perceives that what he reads does not suit his settled tastes, will not break out immediately into violent language and call me a forger and profane person for having the audacity to add anything to the ancient books, or to make any changes or corrections in them?[6]

Two factors, however, prompted Jerome to risk incurring such opprobrium. The first factor, as he related in a dedicatory epistle to Damasus setting forth the occasion and scope of the undertaking, was the command laid upon him by the supreme pontiff. The second was the shocking diversity among the Old Latin manuscripts, there being, as he wrote, "almost as many forms of text as there are manuscripts."

Jerome was born at Strido, a town in Dalmatia near the Adriatic coast, the son of moderately well-to-do Christian parents. His early training was such as to fit him admirably for work as translator, for he received a first-class education in grammar and rhetoric at Rome under the illustrious teacher Aelius Donatus, of

---

6. Jerome, *Letter to Damasus*, which, in many manuscripts of the Vulgate, stands as the preface to his revision of the four Gospels. For a translation of the entire letter, see Philip Schaff and Henry Wace, eds., *Nicene and Post-Nicene Fathers of the Christian Church,* 2d series (Grand Rapids: Eerdmans, n.d.), 6:487–88.

whom he always spoke with great respect. Jerome applied himself with diligence to the study of rhetoric and attended the law courts to hear the best pleaders of the day. He became familiar with the Latin classics and studied Plautus and Terence, Sallust, Lucretius, Horace, Virgil, Persius, and Lucan, with commentaries on them by Donatus and others. These developed his feeling for literary style, and he became a follower of Ciceronian traditions.

In the Greek classics, Jerome was less thoroughly at home. Indeed, it appears that he did not learn Greek at all until he went to Antioch in 373–74, when he was in his late twenties. He shows some acquaintance with Hesiod, Sophocles, Herodotus, Demosthenes, Aristotle, Theophrastus, and Gregory of Nazianzus.

His scholarly tools also came to include the Hebrew language. This he learned with great labor in his mature years, first from a converted but anonymous Jew during Jerome's five years of ascetic seclusion in the Syrian desert of Chalcis (374–79) and afterwards in Bethlehem (about 385) from the Palestinian Rabbi bar-Anina, who, through fear of the Jews, visited him by night. Although Jerome's knowledge of Hebrew was defective, it was much greater than that of Origen, Ephraem Syrus, and Epiphanius, the only other church fathers who knew Hebrew at all. Such was the philological training of the man who was destined to fix the literary form of the Bible of the entire Western Church.

Jerome was a rapid worker. Within a year, he finished his version of the Gospels. There is still some doubt as to whether he worked alone or with helpers. In a letter to the pope, he explained his procedure. He altered the Old Latin text, he said, only when it seemed absolutely necessary, retaining in other cases what had become familiar phraseology. This principle, though by no means rigorously observed throughout, explains inconsistencies in practice (e.g., "high priest" is usually translated in Matthew and Luke by *princeps sacerdotum*, in Mark by *summus sacerdos*, and in John by *pontifex*). Jerome's work on the rest of the New Testament was not quite so thorough; several scholars, in fact, have supposed that it was done by someone else, perhaps by Jerome's follower Rufinus the Syrian.

Among the Old Testament books, Jerome turned his attention first to the Psalter. He made two versions of the Old Latin version of the Psalms by comparing it with the Greek Septuagint. These are known as the Roman (384) and Gallican (387–90) Psalters, because they were introduced into Rome and Gaul respectively.[7] Jerome's final revision of the Psalter was made from the Hebrew, but it never attained general use or popularity.

About the time Jerome produced his Gallican Psalter, he also revised the Latin text of some of the other books of the Old Testament with reference to the Septuagint text as provided in Origen's Hexapla. This work, however, did not satisfy Jerome's scholarly standards, and he resolved to undertake a more thorough revision on the basis of the Hebrew original. This great work occupied him from about the year 390 to 404, and separate books or groups of books were published as they were completed. Whether he managed to complete the entire Old Testament is not clear; at any rate, what is known as the Vulgate translation is far from being a uniform piece of work throughout.

Of course the Old Latin rendering, made from the Septuagint, contained the additional books that over the years had been incorporated into manuscripts of the Greek version of the Old Testament. Jerome's high regard, however, for the *Hebraica veritas* led him to set the books that found a place in the Hebrew canon on a higher level than those that did not. In this way, he anticipated the Reformers' distinction between "canonical" and "apocryphal." Jerome's work on the latter books was by no means as thorough as on the others. Tobit he translated in one day, Judith in one night, both of which he dictated to a scribe in Latin. Other deuterocanonical books remain "untranslated," that is, without revision of the Old Latin text.

The apprehension Jerome expressed to Pope Damasus that he would be castigated for tampering with Holy Writ was not unfounded. His revision of the Latin Bible provoked both criticism and anger, sometimes extraordinarily vehement. Augustine, who was himself not too happy with Jerome's preference for the Hebrew original of the Old Testament over the Greek Septuagint (which Augustine regarded as an inspired version), reports (*Letter* 71) an account of tumult that erupted in a North African church at Oea (modern Tripoli) during the reading of a Scripture lesson

---

7. Jerome's Roman Psalter is still in use in services at St. Peter's Basilica in Rome; the Gallican Psalter is the version of the Psalms included in modern printed editions of the Latin Vulgate Bible—this in spite of the superior accuracy of Jerome's subsequent revision of the Psalter on the basis of the Hebrew text.

from the Book of Jonah in Jerome's unfamiliar rendering. When the congregation heard that Jonah took shelter from the sun under some ivy (*hedera*), with one accord they shouted, "Gourd, gourd" (*cucurbita*), until the reader reinstated the old word lest there be a general exodus of the congregation!

For his part, Jerome defended his work with forthright vigor, referring on occasion to his detractors as "two-legged asses" or "yelping dogs"—persons who "think that ignorance is identical with holiness." In the course of time, however, opposition to the revision subsided, and the superior accuracy and scholarship of Jerome's version gave it the victory. It was a clear case of the survival of the fittest.

For nearly a thousand years, the Vulgate was used as the recognized text of Scripture throughout western Europe. It also became the basis of pre-Reformation vernacular Scriptures, such as Wycliffe's English translation in the fourteenth century, as well as the first printed Bibles in German (1466), Italian (1471), Catalán (1478), Czech (1488), and French (1530).

The Coptic Versions

Coptic is the latest phase in the development of the ancient Egyptian language, which until Christian times was written in hieroglyphs and their derivatives, hieratic and demotic script. But owing to the difficulty of these, Egyptian Christians wrote the native language using twenty-four Greek letters, with the addition of seven signs taken over from a more cursive variety of Egyptian demotic to express sounds that did not exist in spoken Greek. It is this form of Egyptian that is now known as Coptic, and a large number of Greek words pertaining to Christian doctrine, life, and worship were eventually incorporated into it.

Coptic literature is almost exclusively religious. It consists for the most part of translations from Greek and includes versions of the Bible, as well as apocrypha of the Old Testament and of the New Testament, the legends of the apostles, the lives and martyrdoms of the saints, and so on.

The topographical conditions of the thousand-mile-long Nile valley were such as to foster the growth and differentiation of similar but distinct dialects, differing from one another chiefly in phonetics but also to some extent in vocabulary and syntax. The dialects of Coptic in which significant portions of the Scriptures are extant are (1) Sahidic, spoken in the area of Thebes (now Luxor), the chief city of Upper (i.e., southern) Egypt; (2) Bohairic, the dialect of Alexandria and the Western Delta of the Nile and Lower (i.e., northern) Egypt generally; (3) Achmimic, used in the region around Panopolis; (4) sub-Achmimic, which stands between Achmimic and Middle Egyptian; (5) Middle Egyptian, sometimes called the Oxyrhynchite dialect; and (6) Fayyumic, in the district of the Fayyum in Middle Egypt.

Translations into various Coptic dialects were first made in the third or fourth century of the Christian era and subsequently revised. Several fragmentary manuscripts of the Gospels dating from the fourth century survive. Among the Coptic versions, Sahidic is the oldest and in some respects the most important. The major part of the Old Testament, including a fairly complete Pentateuch, can be reconstructed from the considerable number of extant portions of manuscripts. Versions of the Psalms exist in many manuscripts, but the most important is one from the sixth century A.D. that is complete and contains Psalm 151.

Since it is unlikely that there had been any appreciable amount of Judaistic proselytizing that would have called for a translation of the Hebrew Scriptures into Coptic, most scholars agree that the rendering of the Old Testament was made from copies of the Greek Septuagint.

Early in the twentieth century, archaeologists, working near the southern border of the province of the Fayyum, came upon a large collection of manuscripts, almost all of them written in Sahidic. Many of them date from the first half of the ninth to the latter half of the tenth century. The collection, which comprises fifty-six biblical as well as patristic and hagiographical works, was acquired by the Pierpont Morgan Library in New York and has been published in a magnificent facsimile edition of sixty-three volumes. Other famous collections that include Sahidic manuscripts of the Bible are the Chester Beatty collection in Dublin and the Martin Bodmer collection in Cologny-Geneva.

Bohairic is the latest of the several Coptic versions and, in common with the others, shows the influence of the Sahidic. Nevertheless, though it is the latest, this version must form the basis of any study of the Coptic texts. It is the only version that is completely preserved and whose text is attested throughout by several manuscripts. The version ultimately became the accepted Bible in

Egypt, and the dialect survived as the ecclesiastical and liturgical language of the Coptic Church, even after Arabic had been adopted as the speech of everyday life.

A well-preserved early copy of the Gospel according to Matthew in the Middle Egyptian dialect was acquired in the 1950s by the William H. Scheide Library of Princeton. Dated by paleographers to the fourth or fifth century, it is one of the four oldest copies in any language of the entire text of Matthew. Of the other three, Codex Vaticanus and Codex Sinaiticus belong to the fourth century, and Codex Washingtonianus is dated to the fourth or fifth century (codices Alexandrinus and Ephraemi of the fifth century are incomplete in Matthew, and the several Greek and Coptic papyri that antedate the sixth century preserve only scraps of the text of Matthew). Furthermore, the Scheide Matthew is one of the oldest parchment manuscripts to preserve its original binding. This is made of wooden boards, beveled at the edges, with four holes along the binding edge of each board. Portions of leather thongs remain in most of the holes, but the back strip, presumably made also of leather, is gone. It can be appreciated, therefore, that in several respects the Scheide manuscript is of more than ordinary importance.

One of the earliest manuscripts written in the sub-Achmimic dialect is an almost complete copy of the Gospel according to John, now in the library of the British and Foreign Bible Society (kept at Cambridge University). Comprising originally one hundred numbered pages, the codex today has only forty-three leaves or fragments thereof; the text begins at 2:2 on the page numbered 7 and ends at 20:20 on page 96. It is clear, therefore, that six numbered pages (i.e., three leaves of text) are missing at the beginning and at the end of the codex. The handwriting bears a strong resemblance to that of the mid-fourth-century copy of the Greek Bible known as Codex Vaticanus, allowances being made for the fact that one is on papyrus and the other on parchment.

Along with the influence of the Greek Septuagint already indicated, the Coptic versions of the Old Testament frequently show a relationship with the Old Latin versions. For example, the Achmimic version sometimes agrees with the Old Latin against all others, and very rarely does it coincide with the peculiarities of the Bohairic. This is not surprising, because the Old Latin version is regarded as having been of preeminent importance for the African Church.

The Gothic Version

The Goths, an Eastern Germanic people, first entered history in the third century of the Christian era, when they were settled north of the Black Sea. They soon split into two divisions, taking their names from the areas in which they settled. In the fourth century, the Visigoths or West Goths moved farther west under the pressure of the advancing Huns, while the Ostrogoths settled in Pannonia (roughly, modern Hungary), which they received as allies of the Eastern Roman Empire. Prompted by Constantinople, they entered Italy in 458, defeated and slew (493) the barbarian Italian king Odoacer, and set up the Ostrogothic kingdom of Italy, with Ravenna as their capital. During the sixth century, their kingdom was overthrown, and the Ostrogoths gradually lost their identity.

During the fourth century, the Visigoths, who had preceded their Gothic kinsmen into Eastern Europe, peacefully infiltrated Moesia and Dacia (modern Bulgaria and Romania). Here they encountered Christianity, partly as a result of the missionary work of Ulfilas and his translation of the Bible into Gothic. Late in the same century, they began their rampaging migration across southern Europe, eventually conquering Italy and sacking Rome under Alaric in 410. Alaric died soon after, and under Ataulf, the Visigoths left Italy (412) and went into South Gaul and Spain. Their capital was established in Spain, and the Visigoths quietly assimilated the developing Spanish culture and language.

Born about 311, Ulfilas was the son of a Cappadocian captive and a Gothic father, who gave him a typically Gothic name, a diminutive formed from *wulfs*, meaning "little wolf." He spent much of his life as a young man at Constantinople, where he was converted to Christianity. In about 341, he was consecrated bishop by the Arian bishop Eusebius of Nicomedia. Shortly afterwards, he returned to the Visigoths and spent the rest of his life as an ardent missionary bishop and temporal leader.

Ulfilas's greatest accomplishment was twofold: the creation of an alphabet (composed primarily of Greek and Latin characters, but including elements of Gothic runes)[8] and the translation of the

---

8. The Gothic, or "black-letter," type used in printing has no connection with Ulfilas's alphabet, which, to avoid confusion, is termed Moeso-Gothic. This Moeso-Gothic character was used for some of the earlier printings of the surviving Gothic materials.

Scriptures into his native tongue, (Visi)Gothic. It embraced the whole Bible except the books of Samuel and Kings, which he omitted as likely to inflame the military temper of the Gothic race with their records of war and conquests.

It is remarkable that, although nearly one-third of Europe was at that time under the rule of the Goths, next to nothing remains of the Gothic language, which today is extinct. Of the Old Testament, all that has survived are some words from Genesis 5:3–30 and Psalm 52:2–3 and portions of Nehemiah 5–7. As for the New Testament, we have a little less than half of the text of the Gospels and some portions of all the Pauline Epistles (only 2 Corinthians is complete). No portion of Acts, the Epistle to the Hebrews, the General Epistles, or the Apocalypse has survived. With the exception of the famous Codex Argenteus, which will be described in a moment, all the other Gothic texts are palimpsest. That is, after the Gothic language had become extinct, people needing parchment would erase or scrape off the writing (*palimpsest* means "scraped again") and reuse the parchment for some other text—often with remnants of earlier, imperfectly erased writing still visible.

The Codex Argenteus (the Silver Codex) of the early sixth century is a deluxe copy of the four Gospels, written with silver ink on purple parchment. Golden letters lend special splendor to the first three lines of each Gospel. Of the original 336 leaves, each measuring 7 5/8 by 9 7/8 inches, 188 have survived—one leaf having turned up as recently as 1970. The order of the Gospels is the so-called Western order (Matthew, John, Luke, Mark), like that of two fifth-century Greek manuscripts (Codex Bezae and Codex Washingtonianus), a few of the older Peshitta manuscripts, and a considerable number of Old Latin manuscripts. This order seems to have arisen from a desire to give the two apostles a leading place. As for the two who were held to be associated with apostles, the greater length of Luke's Gospel takes precedence over Mark's Gospel.

The fate of the Silver Codex during the first thousand years of its existence is veiled in obscurity. At the middle of the sixteenth century, while resting in the library of the monastery of Werden on the Ruhr in Westphalia, it was brought to the attention of the learned world by two Belgian scholars. Subsequently, the Emperor Rudolph II, who admired objets d'art and manuscripts, took the codex to his favorite castle, the Hradčany in Prague. In 1648, the last year of the Thirty Years War, it was brought to Stockholm as part of the spoils of war and presented to the young queen of Sweden, Christina. After her conversion to Roman Catholicism in 1654 and her necessary abdication of the throne of a Lutheran nation, her learned librarian, the Dutchman Isaac Vossius, was given the manuscript, which then set out on a new journey when Vossius returned to his native land. In 1662 the manuscript was purchased by the Swedish Lord High Chancellor, Count Magnus Gabriel De la Gardie, one of the country's most illustrious noblemen and patrons of art.

As chance would have it, the precious manuscript was almost lost forever when, during a blinding storm, the ship that was carrying it back to Sweden ran aground on one of the islands in Zuider Zee. But careful packing protected it from the effects of the salt water, and the next voyage on another ship was completed successfully. Fully aware of the historic worth of the codex, in 1669 De la Gardie gave it to the library of the university at Uppsala.

In 1927, when Uppsala University celebrated its 450th anniversary, a monumental facsimile edition of the manuscript was produced. A team of photographers, using the most advanced methods of reproduction, succeeded in producing a set of plates of the entire manuscript that are more legible than the faded parchment leaves themselves.

The romantic story of this famous codex has yet another chapter that must be added. In 1970, during the renovation of St. Afra's chapel in the cathedral of Speyer, the diocesan archivist, Dr. Franz Haffner, discovered in a wooden chest of relics a manuscript page that, upon examination, turned out to belong to Codex Argenteus. The leaf preserves the concluding sentences of the Gospel according to Mark (16:12–20).

The Armenian Version

Armenia claims the honor of being the first kingdom to accept Christianity as its official religion. The founder of Armenian Christianity was Gregory the Illuminator (ca. 257–331), an Armenian of royal lineage who had received Christian training at Caesarea in Cappadocia. Toward the end of the third century, he returned to his native land in order to undertake missionary work. Among his converts was Tiridates I, king of Armenia, who then sent out a herald to command all his subjects to adopt Christianity. Thus, by royal edict, Christianity was made the established religion of Armenia and was embraced by the populace through wholesale baptisms.

In his program of evangelism, Gregory was assisted by co-workers from various backgrounds—Armenians trained in Hellenistic culture as well as Armenians under Syrian influence. During this period, before the invention of the Armenian alphabet, books and documents existed only in Greek and Syriac, and their translation was left to oral interpretation. Consequently, it was through such cultural bridges that the Armenians received both Greek and Syriac Christianity, as well as the literature of both these peoples.

The earliest attempt to construct an Armenian alphabet was made by a certain Bishop Daniel. Since he was a Syrian, he probably took the Aramaic alphabet as a pattern. According to the historian Koriun, the alphabet was found to be unsuitable for representing the sounds of the Armenian language. The foundation of Armenian literature, including the translation of the Bible, dates from the early part of the fifth century. The chief promoters of this cultural development were the catholicos (primate) of the Armenian Church, Sahak (ca. 350–439), a descendent of Gregory the Illuminator, and Sahak's friend and helper, Mesrop (Mesrob or Mashtotz, ca. 361–439), who had exchanged a military career for the life of a monk, missionary, and teacher.

At length and with the help of a Greek hermit and calligrapher, Rufanos of Samosata, about A.D. 406 Mesrop succeeded in producing an Armenian alphabet of thirty-six letters, twenty letters coming directly from Greek, twelve others being formed according to a Greek model, and four being taken from Syriac.

After creating the Armenian alphabet, Mesrop gathered about him a band of keen scholars. Sending some of them to Edessa, to Constantinople, and as far as Rome in search of manuscripts of the Scriptures and of ecclesiastical and secular writers, he inaugurated a program of translation that enriched and consolidated Armenian culture. The first book of the Bible that Mesrop translated was the Book of Proverbs, which was followed by the New Testament. With the help of Sahak and perhaps other translators, the rest of the Old Testament was finished about 410–14.

More manuscripts of the Armenian version are extant today than those of any other ancient version, with the exception of the

Latin Vulgate. The earliest dated manuscript is from the ninth century; it is a copy of the four Gospels written in A.D. 887.

Among noteworthy features of the Armenian version of the Bible was the inclusion of certain books that elsewhere came to be regarded as apocryphal. The Old Testament included the *History of Joseph and Asenath* and the *Testaments of the Twelve Patriarchs,* and the New Testament included the *Epistle of the Corinthians to Paul* and a *Third Epistle of Paul to the Corinthians.*

Many other uncanonical writings of the Old Testament are preserved in Armenian manuscripts. These include *The Book of Adam, The History of Moses, The Deaths of the Prophets, Concerning King Solomon, A Short History of the Prophet Elias, Concerning the Prophet Jeremiah, The Vision of Enoch the Just,* and *The Third Book of Esdras* (being chapters 3–14 of Second Esdras in the Apocrypha of the King James Version and including in chapter 7 the lost section of verses 36 to 105).[9]

In view of the influence of both Greek and Syrian Christianity upon the primitive Armenian Church, it is not surprising that diverse opinions have been held concerning the primary base of the Armenian version. Most scholars have been impressed by several types of evidence pointing to a close affinity between the Armenian and the Greek text. Syrian influence, however, can be seen in the circumstance that the early Armenian New Testament included the apocryphal *Third Epistle to the Corinthians,* as did the early Syriac canon.

Another noteworthy feature of Armenian manuscripts in general is the presence in many of them of lengthy colophons, or notes, supplying information on a broad range of topics. Frequently, these comments provide eyewitness or contemporary accounts of historical events that transpired during the production of the manuscript. One such note in an Armenian copy of the Gospels written in A.D. 989 identifies the last twelve verses of the Gospel according to Mark as "of the presbyter Ariston." Some scholars have thought that the words are intended to identify the long ending of Mark (16:9–20) as the work of the Aristion who is men-

9. For the Armenian text with English translation of all of these writings, see *The Uncanonical Writings of the Old Testament Found in the Armenian MSS. of the Library of St. Lazarus,* translated into English by Rev. Dr. Jacques Issaverdens (Venice: Armenian Monastery of St. Lazarus, 1901).

tioned by Papias in the early second century as one of the disciples of the Lord. In any case, more than one hundred Armenian manuscripts of Mark lack the last twelve verses, ending at 16:8.

The Georgian Version

Georgian is a agglutinative language (i.e., words are formed by combining smaller segments of meaning) belonging to the Caucasian group of languages, which bear no discernible relationship to the Semitic, Indo-European, or Ural-Altaic families surrounding them. The country of Georgia, located to the north of Armenia between the Black Sea and the Caspian Sea, was known in antiquity as Iberia, whence is derived the name of the illustrious monastery of Iveron on Mount Athos.

The earliest tradition concerning the introduction of Christianity among the Iberians tells of the missionary work of a Christian slave woman named Nino, who, during the reign of the Emperor Constantine, had been taken captive by Bakur, the pagan king of Georgia. In spite of some legendary details concerning miracles performed by Nino, historians are inclined to accept the date of about the middle of the fourth century for the introduction of Christianity among the Georgians.

How soon after the evangelization of Georgia a translation of the Scriptures was made in the native language is not known exactly. Before a translation could be made in written form, however, the Georgians needed an alphabet of their own. According to Armenian traditions, after St. Mesrop had drawn up an alphabet for his fellow countrymen, he became concerned about the lack of an alphabet among the neighboring Georgian people. After he had invented an alphabet that represented the sounds that occur in that language, King Bakur of Georgia arranged that it should be taught to boys of the lower social classes at various districts and provinces.

Apart from such traditions, however, it is generally accepted that at least the Gospels and some other parts of the New Testament were made available in written form for Georgian Christians by about the middle of the fifth century. During subsequent centuries, this version was revised, perhaps more than once, and traces of such revisions are discernible in terms of both philology and textual criticism.

It is debated whether the translation was made from Greek, Armenian, or Syriac. The oldest manuscripts that are dated in a colophon are of the ninth and tenth centuries, though earlier fragments exist. A feature of Georgian paleography that bears in some measure upon questions of the dating of manuscripts is the style of the script. The Georgians have employed three alphabets: (1) the ecclesiastical majuscule, in general use until the tenth century and sporadically thereafter in manuscripts; (2) the ecclesiastical minuscule, regularly used in theological manuscripts of the eleventh to the nineteenth century; and (3) the "warrior" or "knightly" hand, the ancestor of the modern Georgian script.

A new stage in the history of the spiritual, literary, and cultural life of Georgia began at the close of the tenth century. Noteworthy in this development was St. Euthymius (d. ca. 1028), a scholarly abbot of the Georgian monastery on Mount Athos. In addition to translating various Greek liturgical and homiletical works, St. Euthymius turned his attention to revising and completing the Georgian New Testament. He was the first to translate the Book of Revelation, which for centuries was not regarded as canonical by the Georgian Church. His work must have been completed sometime before A.D. 978, which is the date of the earliest known Georgian manuscript of the Apocalypse.

The Ethiopic Version

The time and circumstances of the planting of the church in Ethiopia are difficult to ascertain. The account in Acts 8:26–39 of the conversion by Philip of an Ethiopian who was chamberlain to the Candace (or queen) of the Ethiopians is often assumed to have a bearing on the introduction of Christianity into Ethiopia. Conflicting traditions in the early church assign the evangelization of Ethiopia to different apostles. The first more or less firm literary evidence we have for the presence of Christianity in Ethiopia comes from the close of the fourth century. According to Rufinus's *Ecclesiastical History* (1.9), it was during the time of Constantine the Great (about 330) that two young men, Frumentius and Ædesius, preached the gospel to residents in Aksum, the capital of Ethiopia. After the royal family had been converted to the new faith, Frumentius went to Alexandria, where he obtained missionary co-workers from Bishop Athanasius and was himself consecrated bishop and head of the Ethiopian Church.

Apart from the credibility of certain details in Rufinus's account, inscriptional and numismatic evidence confirms his central point concerning the arrival of Christianity in Ethiopia during the fourth century. How rapidly the new faith spread among the populace we have no information. There is no indication that the conversion of the king was followed by any royal decree for the enforcement of the faith upon his people.

Concerning the next century and a half, little specific information about the church in Ethiopia has come down to us. Early in the sixth century, a Christian traveler, Cosmas Indicopleustes, visited the country and reported that he found it thoroughly Christianized. The stimulus to growth seems to have come partly because of support given by Christian rulers and partly from encouragement provided by the immigration of Christian believers from other lands. The latter were chiefly Monophysites who, having been condemned at the Council of Chalcedon in 451, were persecuted by Byzantine rulers. They then found refuge in Ethiopia, which, because of its remote geographical location, remained unaffected by religious controversies raging elsewhere.

Noteworthy among the immigrants who helped to evangelize the remaining pagan areas in the northern part of the Aksumite kingdom were monks, nuns, priests, and hermits from Egypt and Syria. Among these newcomers were nine celebrated monks who, because of their vigorous missionary activity and reputation for piety in Ethiopia, have been accorded the status of sainthood. They founded monasteries, developed the liturgy, and made translations of sacred books into the native language.

The question when the Bible, or at least the New Testament, was translated into Ethiopic (or Geʿez, as the Ethiopians call their language) has received the most widely divergent answers, extending at one extreme from the apostolic age to a time after the fourteenth century on the other. All things considered, it is probable that the Ethiopic version was made during the fifth and/or sixth century, in connection with the missionary activity of the Nine Saints.

Of the several thousand Ethiopic manuscripts in European and American collections, about three hundred contain the text of one or more books of the New Testament. Unfortunately, most of these manuscripts are relatively late, dating from the sixteenth to the nineteenth century. The earliest biblical manuscripts come from the fourteenth century. One of the most remarkable Ethiopic manuscripts so far as iconography is concerned is the Pierpont Morgan MS. 828 of the four Gospels, A.D. 1400–1401, with twenty-six full-page miniatures, eight ornamented canon tables, and four ornamented incipit folios.

The Arabic Versions

In antiquity the geographical term *Arabia* encompassed the territory west of Mesopotamia, east and south of Syria and Judea, extending to the Isthmus of Suez. This area, about one-fourth that of Europe and one-third that of the United States, was divided by the geographer Ptolemy into three regions: Arabia Felix (the Happy or Fertile), Arabia Petraea (the Stony), and Arabia Deserta (the Desert). When and how and by whom the gospel was brought to these diverse areas is not known, for the data are scattered and inconclusive.

On at least two occasions during the first half of the third century, Origen was invited to Arabia in order to participate in doctrinal discussions, convened because of certain heretical tendencies on the part of contemporary leaders (Beryllus and Heraclides). At a later date, efforts were made to introduce Christianity among the nomad tribes. It also appears that about the same time Christian missions penetrated the southern part of the Arabian peninsula from Ethiopia.

Who it was that made the first translation of the Scriptures into Arabic is not known. Various traditions have assigned the honor to different persons. The earliest translations probably date from the eighth century. According to an analysis by Ignazio Guidi of more than seventy-five Arabic manuscripts, the Arabic versions of the Gospels existing in manuscripts fall into six basic groups: (1) those made directly from the Greek; (2) those made directly from or corrected from the Syriac Peshitta; (3) those made directly from or corrected from the Coptic (usually the Bohairic dialect); (4) those made from Latin; (5) manuscripts of two distinct eclectic recensions produced by the Alexandrian Patriarchate during the thirteenth century; and (6) miscellaneous manuscripts, some of which are characterized by being cast in the form of rhymed prose made classic by the Koran. Furthermore, more than one Arabic version has been corrected from others derived from a different basic text.

From the Middle Ages to the nineteenth century, other Arabic translations of the Bible were made for various ecclesiastical groups as well as in a variety of forms of Arabic. The former include translations made for Melchites, Maronites, Nestorians, Jacobites, and Copts; the latter include, besides classical Arabic, those forms of the language currently used in Algeria, Chad, Egypt, Morocco, Palestine, Sudan, and Tunisia, as well as the vernacular of Malta.

The Sogdian Version

Sogdian, a Middle Iranian language, was an eastern member of the Indo-European family of languages. During the second half of the first millennium of the Christian era, it was the lingua franca of an extensive area centered on Samarkand and adjacent parts of Central Asia. Early in the twentieth century, a variety of Sogdian documents came to light at Turfan in northwest China. In addition to remains of Manichaean and Buddhist texts, several Christian documents were also found. Among these are fragmentary copies of passages from the Gospels according to Matthew, Luke, and John, as well as several verses of 1 Corinthians and Galatians.

The various Sogdian documents have been assigned to the period from the ninth to the eleventh century. The Christian texts are written in a purely consonantal script resembling Estrangela Syriac. It is thought that the translation was made following the vigorous Nestorian mission in Central Asia during the seventh century.

The Old Church Slavonic Version

During the ninth century, a mission to Moravia (in what is now the Czech Republic) had a profound influence on the cultural development of many Slavic nations. Although the mission failed in the country for which it had been intended, the work eventually produced unexpected results among the Bulgarians, Serbians, Croats, and Eastern Slavs and became the basis of the oldest Christian Slavic culture.

Information concerning the Moravian mission has come down to us most fully in two Slavonic sources entitled *Vita Constantini* and *Vita Methodii*. From these sources, the following can be gleaned concerning the "Apostles to the Slavs," as they came to be called. They were two brothers, native Greeks of Thessalonica, Methodius being born about the year 815, and his younger brother, Constantine, in 826 or 827. Since large numbers of Slavs had settled in the neighborhood of Thessalonica, which was an important outpost of the empire and the second city after Constantinople, the two brothers were acquainted from childhood with the Slavic dialect spoken in the district. The younger brother, having completed his university education at Constantinople, took orders and became librarian of Santa Sophia.

Shortly after the middle of the ninth century, a Moravian prince, Rostislav, sent a petition to the Emperor Michael III ("The Drunkard") of Constantinople, asking for missionaries to instruct his people. The emperor, although more noted for his dissipation than his piety, acceded to Rostislav's request and, perhaps after consulting with the Patriarch Photius, sent Constantine, accompanied by his brother Methodius. Arriving in Moravia about 863, the brothers were received with honor and began the instruction of pupils who were assigned to them. At this time, Constantine translated several liturgical books into Slavonic and also started to train Moravians for the clergy.

Soon afterwards, a controversy developed over the introduction of the Byzantine rite, sung in the language of the Slavs, into a land over which the bishops of Passau and Salzburg claimed spiritual sovereignty. The "theological" base of the argument was that only Greek, Latin, and Hebrew had the right to serve as liturgical languages. In spite of machinations of German priests against Constantine and Methodius, eventually two popes—Hadrian II and John VIII—gave approval for the use of the Slavonic vernacular in divine services. There was, however, one requirement that both pontiffs imposed: the Scripture lessons were to be presented first in Latin and then in the Slavonic translation.

After doing missionary work for several years in Moravia, the two brothers set out for Rome. According to both *Vitae*, Constantine fell ill while in Rome and, sensing that his end was approaching, took monastic vows and assumed the name Cyril. Fifty days later, he died (February 14, 869) and was buried in the basilica dedicated to St. Clement.

Subsequently, Methodius returned to Pannonia (in what is now western Hungary) as archbishop of Sirmium (including, probably, Moravia as well), a province that had lapsed at the time of the Avar invasion in the sixth century. Methodius's new authority came into direct conflict with the Bavarian hierarchy, and the ensuing polemics resulted in his imprisonment for two and a half years. Following his election as pope in 872, John VIII, having become aware of the situation, saw to it that Methodius was released, and the Slavonic liturgy was reinstated in Moravia.

Upon the death of Methodius in 885, the German clergy renewed their efforts to forbid the use of the Slavonic liturgy in Moravia, and the disciples of Methodius were brutally expelled from the country and in some instances sold into slavery. Thus, extinguished in its first home, Slavonic Christianity was carried by these refugees to other Slavic lands.

Attention must now be turned to the invention of the Slavic alphabets and the earliest translation of the Scriptures into Slavonic. According to the *Vita Constantini*, before leaving for Moravia, Cyril devised an alphabet for the writing of Slavonic and began the work of translating the gospel message, beginning with the passage, "In the beginning was the Word, and the Word was with God, and the Word was God" (John 1:1).

The difficulties that the modern philologist faces, however, arise from the fact that the extant Old Church Slavonic manuscripts present us with two distinct alphabets, the Glagolitic and the Cyrillic. Which of the alphabets Cyril invented, the relationship of the two alphabets to each other, and their antecedents, are questions to which widely divergent answers have been given. Today, however, there is widespread agreement that the alphabet invented by Cyril to take to the Moravian Slavs was that now called Glagolitic. The oldest manuscripts in this script date from the late tenth or early eleventh century.

The Cyrillic alphabet is, most scholars agree, of later provenance than the Glagolitic and is based on the Greek uncial script of the ninth and tenth centuries. This alphabet, which is considerably less individualistic than the Glagolitic, may have been devised by St. Kliment, a pupil of Cyril and Methodius and an active missionary in Bulgaria. After some amount of local variation, in 893 a great Bulgarian council held at Preslav not only decreed the general use of the Slavic language in the church but also finally codified the Cyrillic alphabet, making it official for both ecclesiastical and secular use.

The Nubian Version

During the early centuries of the Christian era, Nubia, which lay between Egypt on the north and Ethiopia on the south, comprised three independent kingdoms. When it was that Christianity first reached the Nubian people is not known. Probably Christian influences began to penetrate Nubia from the time that the church became firmly established in Upper Egypt during the third and fourth centuries. During the fourth century, the vast stretches south of Philae would have given shelter to more than one Christian driven from Egypt by the persecutions ordered by the Emperor Diocletian.

The first formally designated missionaries arrived in Nubia about the middle of the sixth century. These belonged to rival factions, the Monophysite and the orthodox Melchite. Questions as to how far each group prospered, what language or languages were used in the liturgies, and whether it is possible to determine from the surviving ruins of churches which form of Christianity prevailed at a given location have been widely discussed and need not detain us here. It is enough to mention that during the succeeding centuries the number of churches in Nubia multiplied and were counted, we are told, by the hundreds. For about five centuries, Christianity flourished, providing the chief cohesive element in Nubian society.

However, by the end of the fourteenth century, having been cut off from the rest of the Christian world by Arab invaders pressing southward from Muslim Egypt, the weakened Nubian Church was ready to expire. The growing power of the Arabs hemmed in the Nubian Christians on the north, east, and west, and finally the whole population apostatized and embraced Islam.

When it was that the Scriptures were translated into Nubian is unknown. If, however, the pattern of evangelization was similar to that in other lands, it is probable that, soon after the introduction of Christianity on a wide scale in the sixth century, a vernacular version would have been called for by the new converts.

It was only in the twentieth century that evidence for the Nubian version came to light. In 1906 Dr. Carl Schmidt purchased in Cairo a quire of sixteen mutilated pages from a parchment codex acquired in Upper Egypt. This contained a portion of a lectionary for Christmastide, corresponding to December 20 to 26. For each day a section of the Scripture is supplied from the Apostolos (Romans, Galatians, Philippians, and Hebrews) and the Gospel (Matthew and John). Except in two instances, the sequence and the choice of the lessons find no parallel in the Greek and Coptic lectionaries hitherto examined. The exceptions involve the two passages appointed for December 25 (Gal. 4:4–7 and Matt. 2:1–12), which coincide with those of Greek menologia (i.e., monthly readings on the lives of the saints).

Like other texts of Nubian, the lectionary is written in an alphabet that is essentially Coptic, reinforced by several additional letters needed to represent sounds peculiar to the language.

Toward the end of the twentieth century, several other biblical fragments in Nubian came to the attention of scholars. These include the Nubian text of verses from the Gospel according to John and the Book of Revelation.[10]

10. For the text of all of the known fragments of the Old Nubian version, see Gerald M. Browne, *Bibliorum sacrorum versio palaeonubiana* (Louvain: Peeters, 1994).

PART 2

English Versions

———

three

English Bibles before the King James Version

The Beginnings of the English Bible

The story of the English Bible begins with the introduction of Christianity into Britain. When and how that happened are obscure, but in the third century Tertullian and Origen witness to the existence of British churches, the former stating that there were places in Britain subject to Christ which Roman arms had not been able to penetrate. Among delegates who attended the Council of Nicaea (A.D. 325) were several from Britain. Although initial developments of the church were wiped out by Teutonic invasions in the fifth century, significant advance began again with the arrival in A.D. 597 of missionaries sent out by Pope Gregory, and Christianity became firmly established.

In Britain, as elsewhere, missionary work proceeded almost entirely by means of the spoken word. Any translation of the

Scriptures consisted of a free and extemporaneous rendering of
the Latin text into the vernacular speech. Interlinear translations
into Old English begin to appear in the ninth and tenth centuries.
Among surviving copies of Anglo-Saxon renderings of the Gospels in various dialects are the famous Lindisfarne Gospels, a
Latin manuscript (now in the British Library) written by Bishop
Eadfrith of Lindisfarne toward the end of the seventh century.
About the middle of the tenth century, a priest named Aldred
wrote between the lines a literal rendering of the Latin in the
Northumbrian dialect. A similar gloss is provided in the Rush-
worth Gospels, a manuscript copied from the Lindisfarne Gospels
and now housed in the Bodleian Library, Oxford. The Rushworth
glosses are practically transcripts of the Lindisfarne glosses so far
as the Gospels of Mark, Luke, and John are concerned, but in
Matthew the Rushworth gloss is an independent rendering in the
rare Mercian dialect by a priest named Farman. A copy of the four
Gospels in West Saxon orthography is preserved at Cambridge
University Library and is generally dated to about A.D. 1050. According to an inscription, the manuscript was given by Bishop Le-
ofric (d. 1072) to his cathedral church at Exeter. In addition to the
four Gospels, the manuscript contains the apocryphal *Gospel of
Nicodemus* and the *Embassy of Nathan the Jew to Tiberius Caesar*, both
in Anglo-Saxon.

The Norman conquest of England (A.D. 1066) marked the end
of the production of Scripture translation into Anglo-Saxon and
Old English. For some three centuries, Norman French largely
supplanted English among educated people; Latin, of course, continued to be used by the clergy. In the fourteenth century, English
translation of parts of the Scriptures began to appear again, the
form of the language being what is now called Middle English.

The Wycliffite Bible (1382; 1388)

So far as we know, the first complete English Bible was due to
the influence and activity of John Wycliffe (c. 1330–84), an eminent Oxford theologian, called the "morning star of the Reformation" because of the religious convictions that he developed and
propagated. In his treatise of 1378, *De Potestate Papae* ("Concerning
the Authority of the Pope"), he maintained that the Bible, as the
eternal "exemplar" of the Christian religion, was the sole criterion

of doctrine, to which no ecclesiastical authority might lawfully add, and that the authority of the pope was ill-founded in Scripture. A strong believer in the Bible as the Word of God addressed to every person, he felt the need to provide the Scriptures in a form that the ordinary reader could use. Interested in both religious and political reform in England, Wycliffe had powerful enemies who finally were able to bring him to trial for heresy. At a synod held at Blackfriars, London, on May 21, 1382, twenty-four theses from his writings and sermons were condemned as heretical or erroneous.

It is doubtful whether Wycliffe himself took any direct part in the work of translating the Scriptures; he died at Lutterworth of a stroke on December 31, 1384. One need not, however, have any qualms about referring to the Wycliffite Bible, for it was under his inspiration that the work was done. In fact, two complete versions of the Scriptures were produced by his pupils and colleagues, John Purvey and Nicholas of Hereford, These were handwritten inasmuch as printing had not yet been invented. The first version, produced about 1382, was extremely literal, corresponding word for word to the Latin, even at the expense of natural English word order. The second version, which appeared about 1388, was more free and shows a feeling for native English idiom throughout. The translation was made from the current Latin Vulgate text and so included the Old Testament apocryphal/deuterocanonical books.

In 1415 the Wycliffite Bible was condemned and burned. Purvey and Nicholas were jailed and forced to recant their teachings. In 1428 Pope Martin V insisted that Wycliffe's body be exhumed, burned, and his ashes cast into the river that flowed through Lutterworth. But just as his ashes were carried by that river to multiple points, so his message went far and wide during the following centuries.

In spite of the zeal with which the hierarchy sought out heresy, about one hundred and eighty copies of the whole or of parts of the Wycliffe versions have survived, mostly dating from before 1450. Of these, fifteen copies of the Old Testament and eighteen copies of the New are of the older version. Just as Martin Luther's version had very great influence upon the German language, so too the Wycliffite Bible was well received by the people and influenced greatly the development of the English language.

The survival of so many manuscripts of the Wycliffite Bible in spite of opposition and destruction indicates its widespread influence which can be credited to the efforts of the "poor priests" or "Lollards" who carried on Wycliffe's work following his death. Replacing a number of similar and fragmentary attempts at translation made in the same period, it remained the only English Bible until the sixteenth century, when printing was invented and newer translations began to be published.[1]

During the first half of the fifteenth century, some copies of this version were augmented by the inclusion following Colossians of the spurious *Letter of Paul to the Laodiceans*. In Colossians 4:16, Paul directs the Colossians, after they have read his letter to them, to pass it on to the church of Laodicea and to see that they in turn have an opportunity to "read also the letter from Laodicea." Although no such letter occurs in the New Testament, before the end of the fourth century someone forged such a composition in Paul's name. This inauthentic letter circulated in Latin for many centuries and sometimes was included in manuscripts of the Latin Vulgate.

Tyndale and the First Printed English New Testament (1526)

With the sixteenth century, we enter a new era in the history of the Bible in English. The Scriptures were made known in their original languages; the first printed Hebrew Bible was issued in 1488, and the first published Greek New Testament, an edition of Erasmus, in 1516. Scholars like Erasmus and reformers like Luther worked for the right of all to read the sacred text.

At this time, William Tyndale, born about 1492 and educated at Oxford and Cambridge in Greek and Hebrew, came upon the scene. While still a young man, he conceived the idea of making a new and better English version of the Bible, based on the original languages. About 1523 he sought help and encouragement from the bishop of London in the production of such a version but was vigorously rebuffed. The next year, having decided that it would

---

1. The first printed edition of the complete Wycliffite Bible did not appear until 1850, when Josiah Forshall and Frederic Madden issued the earlier and the later versions, printed side by side in four volumes (Oxford University Press).

be virtually impossible to do what he had in mind anywhere in England, he left England for Hamburg, never to return.

While in Germany, he found it necessary in order to escape interference to move from place to place several times. Despite such interruptions, by the middle of 1525 his translation of the New Testament was complete, and printing was begun at Cologne. A quarto edition was interrupted by the authorities at the instigation of a bitter enemy of the reformers, Cochlaeus (Johannes Dobeneck). From it only a fragment of Matthew (thirty-one leaves) is extant, although it is believed that three thousand copies were published after the work was resumed at Worms. Here also an anonymous octavo edition was first published. So vigorous was the opposition of the English authorities, however, and so zealously did kings and bishops collaborate to destroy the Tyndale publications as they were being smuggled into England that only four copies of the original 1526 edition and the revisions of 1534 and 1535 are known to have survived, and one of these is very fragmentary.

Antwerp, which was Tyndale's residence in his closing years, was a free city, but the surrounding territory was under the control of Charles V, the Holy Roman Emperor. Tyndale's enemies could take no legal action against him in Antwerp; but in the emperor's domains, it would be easy to proceed against him for heresy. On May 21, 1535, through the treachery of a young Englishman named Henry Phillips, he was kidnapped, conveyed out of Antwerp, and imprisoned in the fortress of Vilvorde, some six miles north of Brussels.

Tyndale also worked on a translation of the Hebrew Old Testament but was unable to complete it before his death. He published the Pentateuch in 1530 and Jonah in 1531. There is evidence that he translated other portions of the Old Testament besides those already mentioned, most probably to the end of 2 Chronicles with several prophetical books, but he did not live to publish them.

Tyndale's translation of the Old Testament is free, bold, and idiomatic. The serpent says to Eve in Genesis 3:4, "Tush, ye shall not die"; in Genesis 39:2 we read that "the Lorde was with Joseph, and he was a luckie felowe"; in Exodus 15:4 Pharaoh's "jolly captains" are drowned in the Red Sea; and in verse 26 of the same chapter God introduces himself as "the Lord thy surgeon."

After an imprisonment of a year and a half (during which time he probably completed his translation through Chronicles), he was tried for heresy and convicted. On October 6, 1536, he was put to death by strangling and his body burned. His last words were "Lord, open the king of England's eyes."

Meanwhile, before his death the situation in England had already changed for the better under Thomas Cromwell, who had even sought Tyndale's release. A complete English Bible, based largely on Tyndale's work but without his name, was now being circulated and read in England openly and with King Henry's permission.

Tyndale's version is important not only because it was a pioneer effort in translating the Scriptures from the original languages into English, but also because of the great influence it had upon later translations. Its simplicity and directness mark the work as a truly great achievement in literature, apart from its epoch-making religious importance. It became, in fact, a foundation for all subsequent efforts of revision, so much so that 80 percent or more of the English Bible down through the Revised Version has been estimated to be his in those portions of the Bible on which he had worked with such skill and devotion.

Coverdale and the First Complete Printed Bible in English (1535)

The publication of the first complete printed English Bible was the work of Miles Coverdale (1488–1568), a native of York. After becoming a priest, he developed a consuming passion for learning, especially in the field of biblical studies. He apparently found it discreet to spend some years outside of England because of his Protestant convictions. Here he became acquainted with Tyndale and his work and may have been encouraged to attempt a complete edition of the Scriptures in English. The edition that he published in 1535, printed perhaps at Cologne or Marburg, was not authorized in any way, but Coverdale dedicated it to the king and queen in polite and flattering phraseology, and it met with no serious opposition. This toleration is particularly noteworthy because Tyndale's translation was the basis of the rendering of Coverdale's New Testament and Pentateuch.

The Vulgate rather than the Hebrew order of books was used in the Old Testament, and for the first time, the books of the Apocrypha were separated from the other Old Testament books and printed by themselves as an appendix to the Old Testament—a precedent followed by English Protestant Bibles ever since (insofar as they include the Apocrypha at all). In the New Testament, the two epistles of Peter and the three of John come before the Epistle to the Hebrews, which is followed by James, Jude, and Revelation. This order of books is the same as in Luther's and Tyndale's versions.

In general, the Tyndale portions of the edition are superior in quality, but Coverdale occasionally improved the phrasing by reason of a special aptitude for euphonious English and for a fluent, though frequently diffuse, form of expression. While the work is uneven in this respect, some permanent contribution was made to the language of the English Bible. Phraseology that appeared first with Coverdale includes "Thou enoyntest my heade with oyle"; "the valley of the shadowe of death"; "but the way of the ungodly shall perish." Coverdale's version of the Psalter was taken over in the Great Bible of 1539, which was reproduced in the Bishops' Bible of 1568, and remained a part of the Anglican Book of Common Prayer until a revision of the latter in the twentieth century.

Matthew's Bible (1537)

Although the title page of the 1537 Bible identifies the translator as Thomas Matthew, there is reason to think that this was a pseudonym intended to veil the identity of the real translator. The work is generally attributed to a man named John Rogers, a Cambridge graduate and friend of Tyndale. He had come into possession of some of Tyndale's unpublished translations of several Old Testament books. Published perhaps at Antwerp, the translation follows closely the Tyndale version. A new preface was provided for the Apocrypha, and, as in Coverdale's Bible, the books of the Apocrypha were placed by themselves in an appendix to the Old Testament. The Matthew Bible had, for the first time in English, a translation of the apocryphal Prayer of Manasseh, rendered from the French of Olivétan's Bible.

During Edward VI's short reign (1547–53), Rogers was in favor and given London preferments, and immediately after the king's death, he preached at St. Paul's Cross, warning the people against popery. By January 1554, after Mary had established her claim to the throne, Rogers was in prison, and in February 1555 he was burned alive at Smithfield, the first of the Protestant martyrs. The French ambassador wrote that Rogers died with such composure that it might have been a wedding.

Taverner's Bible (1539)

Richard Taverner, born about 1505, a student at Cambridge and Oxford universities, became a lawyer while continuing his interest in the English Bible by producing a minor revision of Matthew's Bible. Possessing a good knowledge of Greek, he was in a position to translate the Apocrypha for himself; his version, especially of 1 and 2 Esdras, Tobit, and Judith, differs greatly from the versions by Coverdale and by Matthew. The Psalms are numbered as in the Vulgate, and Taverner has four books of Kings, not two of Samuel and two of Kings. The order of books in his version of the New Testament is the same as in Matthew's Bible.

Taverner was a client and pensioner of Thomas Cromwell, who in 1536 appointed him clerk of the Privy Seal. The fall of his patron in 1540 put a stop to his literary work and made his position unsafe. For a time he was imprisoned in the Tower of London because of his activity in the translation and revision of the English Bible. He succeeded, however, in regaining the royal favor, and under Edward VI in 1552, was granted a general license to preach, though a layman. He died in 1575.

Although his version was almost immediately eclipsed by another revision, it does have the honor of being the first to be printed completely in England.

The Great Bible (1539)

The term "great" comes from the size of the volume, which was the largest of the English Bibles yet published (pages measured fifteen by ten inches). It was the first "authorized" English Bible, and in the 1540 and subsequent editions, it carried on the title page the explicit words "This is the Byble apoynted to the use of the churches." It was undertaken by Coverdale at Thomas Cromwell's suggestion and was produced mainly by the revision of the text of Matthew's Bible.

Coverdale did not remain content with the first edition of the Great Bible; he continued his work of revision, and when a second edition appeared in April 1540, it represented a considerable advance over the first edition, especially in the poetical sections of the Old Testament. Six further editions were issued between July 1540 and December 1541.

In the New Testament, Luther's sequence of the books (followed by Tyndale, Matthew, and Coverdale in his 1535 Bible), which places Hebrews, James, Jude, and Revelation at the end in a category by themselves, was discontinued. The order adopted in the Great Bible is that given by Erasmus in his Greek New Testament, and this order was followed by the principal English versions after 1539.

Because of political changes in England, the several editions of the Great Bible had a varied reception. At one time it was ordered placed in churches, at another time ordered removed, and then later again ordered placed. In 1543 restrictions were put upon the reading of the Bible, and in 1546 a general burning of Bibles commenced. The authorized Great Bible alone was allowed, and its reading was limited to the upper classes. With the death of Henry on January 28, 1547, Protestants were again at liberty, during the six years of the youthful Edward's reign, to resume their interrupted production of biblical translations.

Edmund Becke's Bibles (1549; 1551)

In the short reign of Edward VI, the open Bible came once again into favor, and some fourteen Bibles and thirty-five New Testaments were printed. These were reprints of Tyndale, Matthew, and Taverner, some of them of interest only for the light they throw on the liberties that publishers felt free to take with books and parts of books in producing a "hybrid" edition. One such printer/publisher was Edmund Becke, who also tried his hand at some desultory revising. Occasionally called "Bishop Becke's Bibles," these comprise essentially Taverner's Old Testament and Tyndale's New Testament, compiled by John Daye and revised and edited by Becke.

The edition of 1549 is printed in a rather peculiar black-letter type in double columns. The majority of the notes are gathered together after the chapter to which they pertain. Present also are

Tyndale's prologues, including the long prologues to Jonah and Romans (eleven pages) and that to the New Testament.

The edition of 1551 includes 3 Maccabees in the Apocrypha. A cut of the Evangelist appears before each Gospel, and at the beginning of the dedication stands a woodcut initial, representing Becke offering his book to the young king, Edward VI, and instructing him in the duties of his high station.

Becke's alterations in this edition of the New Testament are deplorable. By reverting in nearly every instance to Tyndale's version, he has done injustice to Taverner by perpetuating mistakes that the latter had corrected.

Both editions contain the notorious "wife-beater" note on 1 Peter 3:7, where men are exhorted to live with their wives "according to knowledge." Becke explains this to mean

> that taketh her as a necessary helper, and not as a bond servaunt or bonde slave. And if she be not obedient and healpeful unto hym: endeavoureth to beate the feare of God into her heade, that therby she maye be compelled to learne her dutye and do it. But chiefly he must beware that he halte not in anye parte of hys dutye to her warde.[2] For hys evyll example shall destroye more than all entruccions he can give shall edifye.

The Geneva Bible (1560)

Roman Catholic ascendancy and persecution under Mary (1553–58) made further Bible translation and publication in England virtually impossible. English Protestant scholars fled to Switzerland for safety and gathered at Geneva, the headquarters of the Reformed type of Protestantism. Although no names of the translators appear in the Geneva New Testament, which was published by Conrad Badius at Geneva in 1557, the work is mainly credited to William Whittingham, a brother-in-law of John Calvin,[3] who was an able scholar and the successor of John Knox as minister to the English congregation at Geneva. The Old Testament, which was translated by a group including Anthony Gilby,

---

2. I.e., toward her.

3. He married Calvin's wife's sister, according to a note by W. A. Wright in B. F. Westcott's *General View of the History of the English Bible*, 3d ed. (New York: Macmillan, 1916), p. 90.

Thomas Sampson, and others of uncertain identity, was published in 1560, together with a careful revision of the New Testament. From the translation in Genesis 3:7 ("They sewed figge-tree leaves together and made themselves breeches"), the Geneva Bible is sometimes called the "Breeches" Bible.[4]

The Geneva version was equipped with copious notes in the margins, most of which were explanations of difficult points in the text, such as historical and geographical references. Some of the notes were doctrinal and some hortatory. As might be expected, the notes were Calvinistic in tone. When the Geneva Bible was first published, Calvin was the ruling spirit in Geneva, and the features of his theological, ecclesiastical, political, and social system are accordingly reflected in the marginal annotations of the English Bible issued in the city of his residence.

Royalty and clergy, however, and especially Roman Catholic circles, were disturbed by certain of the interpretations. A note on Exodus 1:19, approving of the midwives' lying to Pharaoh, was considered a reflection on royal prerogatives.[5] Roman Catholics naturally objected to identifying the pope with "the angel of the bottomless pit" (Rev. 9:11).[6] One of the reasons that led King James, in 1604, to agree readily to a new translation of the Scriptures was his dislike of the politics preached in the margins of the Geneva Bible.

A number of novel features contributed to the usefulness and popularity of this Bible. Instead of heavy, black-letter type, roman type was used for the first time. It was the first English Bible with numbered verses, which became the basis of all versification in later English Bibles. The practice of italicizing English words not represented in the original text was introduced from Paginus's Latin Bible and Beza, a practice that was to continue down through the Revised Version. The convenient quarto size and consequently cheaper price also contributed to its popularity. Besides

---

4. The translation "brechis" also occurs in the same verse in Wycliffite Bibles, which circulated only in manuscript copies until 1850, when both forms of this version were first printed (see under "Wycliffite Bible" above).

5. The annotation is in two parts: "Their disobedience herein was lawfull, but their dissembling euill."

6. The annotation reads, "Which is Antichrist the Pope, king of hypocrites, and Satans ambassadour."

the marginal annotations, it included a variety of other helps, such as maps, tables, woodcuts, chapter summaries, and running titles. An argument is prefixed to each book. The Hebrew names are carefully spelled and accented (for example Iaakób, Izhák, Rebekáh).

As a result of these various features and the superior and attractive character of the version itself, the Geneva Bible enjoyed an immediate and widespread reception and usage. From 1560 to 1616, not a year passed without a new edition. In 1599 no fewer than ten editions were issued. It was the Bible of Shakespeare, John Bunyan, Cromwell's army, the Puritan pilgrims to the New World, and even (!) of King James himself. About 180 editions of various kinds, 96 complete, were published, 8 of them appearing after the publication of the King James Version in 1611.[7]

The Bishops' Bible (1568)

The popularity and superiority of the Geneva Bible were irksome to the church and state alike, and the Great Bible of 1539 was unable to maintain a position commensurate with its official prerogatives. Consequently, in 1564 Matthew Parker, archbishop of Canterbury, initiated the effort to produce a revision of the Bible that might supplant the Genevan and other versions. Since all the revisers were bishops or eventually became bishops, the new version was naturally called "The Bishops' Bible." The Great Bible was used as the basis of their work, and there was to be only such necessary variation from it as was required by the Hebrew or Greek.

After about four years of work, the first edition was issued in 1568 in a very large and impressive folio. The customary black-letter type was employed, and roman type served the function of the italics that had been used in the Geneva Bible. The New Testament was on thicker paper, to withstand wear. A novel feature of this version was the placing of the translator's initials at the end of the section(s) he had revised; but this was not done consistently. The idea was that such publicity would make the contributors "more

7. For a fuller account of the Geneva Bible, celebrating the tercentennial of its publication, see the present writer's article, "The Geneva Bible of 1560," *Theology Today* 17 (1960): 339–52.

diligent, as answerable for their doings." Passages containing genealogies "or other such places not edifying" were marked so that the lector would omit them in public reading. Extensive supplementary equipment included tables of contents, a chronology, lists of genealogies, maps, pictures, an almanac, numerous decorative woodcuts, two engravings, and marginal annotations. Among the latter were many taken over from the Geneva Bible.[8]

The product is of uneven quality, due to the exercise of individual freedom by the translators without adequate editorial supervision of the whole work. While some sections are therefore close to the Great Bible, especially in the Old Testament and Apocrypha, others depart freely from it. In spite of its defects, the Bishops' Bible became the second "authorized" English version, and eventually it displaced the Great Bible as the one "appoynted to be read in the Churches."[9]

The Rheims-Douay Bible (1582–1610)

Religious persecution, which, under Mary Tudor, had sent English Protestants into exile at Geneva, subsequently, under Elizabeth I, caused English Catholics to find refuge in Flanders. Prominent among Catholics fleeing the wrath of the Virgin Queen was William Allen (afterwards Cardinal Allen), principal of St. Mary's Hall (Oriel College), Oxford, through whose efforts there was established in 1568 at Douay a Catholic seminary for the training of English priests. The Douay scholars undertook, for the first time in the history of the Roman Church, to replace the available Anglican and Genevan Bibles—unacceptable from their point of view—with an English version of their own. This project, under the leadership of the Jesuit scholar Gregory Martin, another Oxonian exile, was completed in 1582 at Rheims in France, to which

8. Exceptional to the Bishops' Bible is the comment on the gold of Ophir in Psalm 45:9: "Ophir is thought to be the Iland in the west coast, of late founde by Christopher Columbo: from whence at this day is brought most fine gold."

9. From 1568 to 1602, the Bishops' Bible went through twenty editions. The New Testament was again printed in 1617 and 1633. The instructions to the King James revisers were that they were to follow the Bishops' Bible where it was true to the original. Actually, however, it owes only an estimated four percent of its wording to the Bishops' text.

city the college had transferred itself in 1578 in order to escape the consequence of Allen's political activities.

Political difficulties, it seems, could be avoided more readily than financial; for, owing to "lacke of good meanes to publishe the whole," only the New Testament portion was put through the press at Rheims, although the entire Bible had been translated. By 1609–10, funds for the publication of the Old Testament in two volumes had become available. By this time, the college had moved back to Douay, and the version is therefore known as the Douay or Rheims-Douay Bible.[10]

The translation, which was made not from the original languages but from the Latin Vulgate, was painstaking and reached a high standard of consistency, but was often too literal to be suitable for use in public worship. There was also a strong tendency to retain technical words (for example, pasch, parasceve, scenopegia, azymes) without alteration. Many passages of so-called English need translating into English by the help of the Latin: "supersubstantial bread" (Matt. 6:11); "odible to God" (Rom. 1:30); "if thou be a prevaricator of the law, the circumcision is become prepuce" (Rom. 2:25); "evacuated from Christ" (Gal. 5:4); "he exinanited himself" (Phil. 2:7); "coiquination and spottes, flowing in delicacies" (2 Pet. 2:13).

In order to enable the ordinary reader to comprehend technical and theological terms, Gregory Martin provided a glossary at the end of the New Testament containing "the explication of certain words in this translation, not familiar to the vulgar reader, which might not conveniently be uttered otherwise."[11]

It is, however, unfair to dwell on this negative though real side of the Rheims version. There is also a positive side. To counterbalance the inflated and Latinate diction, there are many instances of plain colloquial expression and clear rendering: "have a good heart" (Matt. 9:2); "throttled him" (Matt. 18:28); "We never saw

10. In 1667 Louis XIV of France seized Douay, which henceforth was known as Douai. Consequently, the version is now often called the Douai Bible.

11. The Rheims New Testament exerted a very considerable influence on the version of 1611, transmitting to it not only an extensive vocabulary, but also numerous distinctive phrases and terms of expression; see J. G. Carleton's exhaustive analysis, *The Part of Rheims in the Making of the English Bible* (Oxford: Clarendon, 1902).

the like" (Mark 2:12); "Why make you this a doe? the wench is not dead, but sleepeth" (Mark 5:39); and "the stipends of sinne, death" (Rom. 6:23).

The dogmatic intentions of the translators found expression in the preface and in the notes that accompany the text. Annotations in the form of marginalia and notes at the end of chapters rival those in the Geneva Bible in profuseness and exceed it in polemic nature. The Protestant "hereticks" and the Genevan commentators in particular are constantly in mind. The note on Matthew 6:24, for example, gives as the first interpretation of "two masters": "Two religions, God and Baal, Christ and Calvin, Masse and Communion, the Catholike Church and Heretical Conventicales."

From time to time after 1612, the Rheims-Douay Bible received some slight revision, but by the middle of the eighteenth century, its literalistic Latinate rendering was largely unintelligible to the rank and file of English-speaking Roman Catholics. Consequently, Bishop Richard Challoner, the vicar apostolate of the London district, assisted in making a thorough revision of the New Testament in 1738. In the following years, with indefatigable labor, Challoner revised the Old Testament twice, in 1750 and 1763, while doing the same for the New Testament no fewer than five times, in 1749, 1750, 1752, 1763, and 1772. The two Testaments were united by Challoner in a five-volume edition published at London in 1749–50 (3d ed., rev. 1752).

four

The King James Bible

*He did NOT (1611)
write the Bible*

In 1603 when King James VI of Scotland became King James I of England, the text of the Bible, current in a variety of English translations, was a source of division among religious parties in England rather than a bond of unity. In order to reconcile differences among the various parties, the king called for a conference to be held in January 1604 at Hampton Court. Both bishops and Puritan clergy alike were invited to consult together on the subject of religious toleration.

After much inconclusive debate, Dr. John Reynolds, president of Corpus Christi College, Oxford, and spokesman for the Puritan party, raised the subject of the imperfections of the current English Bibles and proposed that a new, or at least a revised, translation be made. The particular objections which he mentioned were neither numerous (only three passages were referred to: Ps. 105:28; 106:30; Gal. 4:25) nor important, and we must conclude either that this part of the Puritans' case had not been carefully thought out or that the bullying to which they were exposed had had the desired effect of throwing them into some confusion. The bishops treated the difficulties which they did raise with supercilious scorn; they were "trivial, old, and often answered." Bishop Bancroft, a stern opponent of the Puritans, raised the objection that "if every man's humour were to be followed there would be no end of translating."

Although the conference itself arrived at no conclusion on this or any other subject, King James, who had a personal interest in biblical study and translation, endorsed the idea of a new translation, stating that none of the existing English versions was translated well, and in his opinion the Geneva Bible was the worst of them all. Whatever his motives, James supported the project so vigorously that by July 1604 a translation committee of some fifty "learned men" and a list of rules of procedure had been provided.

The rules of procedure specified that the Bishops' Bible was to be followed and "as little altered as the truth of the original will permit"; that certain other translations should be used where they agreed better with the text, namely, "Tindoll's, Matthew's, Coverdale's, Whitchurch's [= the Great Bible, so named from the name of the printer], and Geneva"; that "the Old Ecclesiastical Words [were] to be kept, viz. the Word *Church* not be translated *Congregation*, &c."; and that no marginal notes were to be used except for necessary explanation of Hebrew or Greek words. Most of the remaining fifteen rules dealt with method of procedure.

James himself appears to have taken a leading role in organizing the work of the translation. Six panels of translators had the work divided among them; the Old Testament was allotted to three panels, the New Testament to two, and the Apocrypha to one. Two of the panels met at Oxford, two at Cambridge, and two at Westminster. When any panel had finished the revision of a book, it was to be sent to all the rest for their criticism and suggestions, ultimate differences of opinion to be settled at a general meeting of the chief members of each panel.

Beginning probably some time in 1609, and continuing daily for nine months, John Bois, Andrew Downes, and four others went daily to Stationers' Hall in London to review the first draft of the Bible as it came from the panels in the universities and at Westminster. For this intensive labor, each of them received from the Company of Stationers thirty shillings weekly. No previous financial payments had been made to the translators.

The payment for revision brings up the larger question of the cost of the work. Neither king nor parliament had much money to spare, but those who were not already holders of an ecclesiastical benefice were not forgotten when these fell vacant. The payment to the revisers was probably only a small part of the cost of printing and publication. In 1651 it was revealed that Robert Barker, the publisher, had paid thirty-five hundred pounds for the completed and corrected manuscript of the Bible. This manuscript no longer exists, having probably perished in the great fire of London.

The team of revisers was a strong one. It included the professors of Hebrew and Greek at both universities, with practically all the leading scholars and divines of the day. There is a slight uncertainty about some of the names, and some changes in the list may have been caused by death or retirement, but the total number of the revisers was from forty-eight to fifty.[1]

One of the most illustrious of these "learned men" was Lancelot Andrewes, who had begun the study of Greek at the age of six. Eventually, he became acquainted with so many languages that, so it was said, had he been present at the tower of Babel, he could have served as interpreter general! Andrewes is still known today for his famous devotional classic, *Preces Privatae*, a collection of prayers, mainly in Greek, compiled for his personal use; it has several times been translated into English. Two of the other translators, John Bois (Boys) and Andrew Downes, had begun to learn Hebrew at the age of five.

The work, begun in 1607, had taken the incredibly short time of two years and nine months of strenuous toil to prepare for the press. Beyond the royal authority under which it was made and the statement on the title page "Appointed to be read in churches," it had never been officially authorized by ecclesiastical or legislative sanction. In the long run, however, the popularity

---

1. For an account of what is known of the lives of the individual translators, see the research of Gustavus S. Paine, a reporter for the *Christian Science Monitor*. His book, *The Learned Men* (New York: Crowell, 1959), was later reprinted by Baker Book House as, *The Men behind the King James Version*. Another informative account is Olga S. Opfell's *The King James Bible Translators* (Jefferson, N.C., and London: McFarland, 1982).

attained eventually by the version "authorized" it in the national mind—but in a sense different from the authorization of the Great Bible of 1539 and the Bishops' Bible of 1568.

The preliminary matter of the volume included a four-page dedication of the translators' work "to the most high and mighty Prince, James." It is couched in the customary language of fulsome praise: "Upon the setting of that bright occidental Star, Queen Elizabeth," men feared lest religious chaos should darken the land, but "the appearance of Your Majesty, as of the *Sun* in his strength," dissipated their fears. At the close, the translators pray that the king will support them in the work they have completed, "so that if, on the one side, we shall be traduced by Popish persons at home or abroad," who "desire still to keep the people in ignorance and darkness; or if, on the other side, we be maligned by self-conceited brethren, . . . we may rest secure."

Following the dedication (which continues to be printed in the forefront of most British editions of the version) was a much more interesting eleven-page preface of the translators. This superb essay, written probably by Miles Smith, begins in a leisurely and learned fashion, justifying the principle of Bible translation. It then goes on to declare the necessity of this new rendering, explaining that it is a revision, not a new translation, and that the revisers, who had the original Hebrew and Greek texts before them, steered a course between the Puritan and Roman versions. Unfortunately, modern editions of the King James Bible usually omit this preface, thus depriving the reader of the orientation originally provided concerning the purpose of the translators and their procedures and principles.[2]

There were two matters of editorial policy that the translators wished to make clear to the reader. The first concerned the use of marginal notes where there is uncertainty about the wording of the original text or about its interpretation. Although the translators were aware that some persons might fear that such notes

2. In 1997 the American Bible Society issued *The Translators to the Reader* in booklet format with the subtitle *The Original Preface of the King James Version of 1611 Revisited*. Edited by Erroll F. Rhodes and Liana Lupas, it provides a facsimile of the preface; this is followed by a transcription in modern orthography with explanatory notes; and thirdly, a slightly abbreviated form accommodates the text to modern American usage.

would bring into question the authority of the Scriptures, they were convinced that such notes were necessary. They argued that "God had been pleased in his divine providence to scatter here and there words and sentences that are difficult and ambiguous, [which] do not touch on doctrinal points that have to do with salvation, but on matters of less importance." In such instances, "we should be diffident rather than confident, and if we must make a choice, choose modesty with St. Augustine, who recognized that 'It is better to be reserved about things that are not revealed, than to fight about things that are uncertain.'"

The second matter concerned the degree of verbal variety or uniformity to be adopted in translating. In the preface, the translators vindicate the practice of variety (in which they indulge very freely) of translating one word in the original by many English words, partly on the intelligible ground that it is not always possible to find one word that will express all the meanings of the Greek or Hebrew, partly on the somewhat childish plea that it would be unfair to choose some words for the high honor of being the channels of God's truth and to pass over others as unworthy.

The self-imposed law of fairness that led the translators to permit as many English words as possible to share in the honor of representing one word in the Hebrew or Greek text has, as might be expected, marred the excellence of their work. Sometimes the effect is simply the loss of the solemn emphasis of the repetition of the same word. Sometimes it is more serious and affects the meaning. An extreme example is *katargeō*, occurring twenty-seven times in the New Testament and rendered in eighteen different ways, as "abolish, cease, cumber, deliver, destroy, do away, become (make) of no (none, without) effect, fail, loose, bring (come) to naught, put away (down), vanish away, make void." Certainly, the translator must not be peremptorily debarred from the skillful and appropriate choice of the right synonym in the right context, but there are times when the recurrence of the same word is exactly what is required.

Side by side with this fault, there is another just the opposite of it. One English word is used to render several Greek or Hebrew words, and thus shades of meaning, often of importance to the right understanding of the passage, are obscured. Thus, the translators make the one word "trouble" serve for a dozen different

Greek words; one word "bring" to represent thirty-nine Hebrew words; one word "destroy" to represent forty-nine Hebrew words. Sometimes the variation may be attributed to different revisers, especially in the treatment of proper names, sometimes following the Hebrew form, sometimes the Greek, and sometimes even the Latin; as Jeremiah, Jeremias, and Jeremy, Tyrus and Tyre, Elijah and Elias, Noah and Noe, Elisha and Eliseus, Hosea and Osee, Isaiah and Esaias, Korah and Core, Hezekiah and Ezekias, Marcus and Mark, Lucas and Luke, Sinai and Sina, Jonah and Jonas, Judas and Jude, Agar and Hagar.

The historic edition that issued from the press of Robert Barker was a large folio volume, measuring 16 by 10 1/2 inches, very similar to the Bishops' Bible in appearance. The black-letter type and the chapter and verse division were essentially the same. Running titles and prefatory chapter summaries were included, many reflecting the influence of the Geneva Bible. There were several tables and charts. The apocryphal books were given between the testaments without any distinguishing comments. An elaborate engraved title page described the version as "The Holy Bible, Conteyning the Old Testament, and the New: Newly Translated out of the Originall tongues: & with the former Translations diligently compared and revised, by his Maiesties speciall Commandement. Appointed to be read in Churches. Anno Dom. 1611."

The printing history of the King James Version is of particular interest. Three folio editions appeared in 1611, among which were more than two hundred variations in the biblical text. The earliest of the three is known as "the great 'He' edition" and the other two as "the great 'She' editions," because the first renders the closing words of Ruth 3:15 "and he went into the city," whereas the others have "and she went into the city" (the Hebrew manuscripts themselves are divided between "he" and "she"). The editors who passed the printing through the press were Miles Smith of Brasenose College, Oxford, and Thomas Bilson, bishop of Winchester.

In the original printing, the number of marginal references to corresponding passages, including those in the Apocrypha, was about nine thousand. Large as this number may seem, it is but a small fraction of the references in some well-edited modern Bibles. These references doubtless have their value, but it cannot be denied that some of them obscure the meaning of the statements to which they are attached.[3] It is different, however, with what are called the marginal notes, which in the original printing were nearly as numerous as the marginal references. These notes are brief and non-polemical, differing in these respects very markedly from the annotations in both Matthew's and the Geneva Bible. They indicate, for the most part, alternative or more literal renderings. In some cases, they specify variant readings in the original text; in other cases, they give brief explanations of words or expressions.

The final editors had also to regularize punctuation and decide questions of grammar, unless they were able to find helpers for such work, which today would be called "copyediting." Some points of grammar in the King James Bible have bothered readers more than they did the men of 1611, who, like the Elizabethans, wrote with the freedom of a language still more or less fluid. The question in Matthew 16:13, "Whom do men say that I the Son of man am?" violates English grammar. So does the colloquial "It's him," yet many today are ready to accept it, though here *him* is a usage comparable to the *whom*. With their feeling for sound, it is possible that the translators considered "whom do" less objectionable than "who do . . . ?" Occasionally, the wrong pronoun gives a comic effect. In 1 Kings 13:27, the 1611 Bible says "And he spake unto his sons, saying, Saddle me the ass. And they saddled *him*." The "him" is in italics to indicate that is not in the original Hebrew, so there can be no argument when subsequent versions change "him" to "it."

The aim of the revisers is clearly stated in the preface. It was not to make "a new translation, nor yet to make of a bad one a good one . . . but to make a good one better, or out of many good ones one principal good one." Although usually called a translation,[4] it is in fact merely a *revision* of the Bishops' Bible, as this itself was a revision of the Great Bible, and the Great Bible a revision of Coverdale and Tyndale. A great deal of the praise, therefore, that is given to it belongs to its predecessors. For the idiom and vocab-

3. Beyond such occasional obscurities, however, in the 1611 Bible the references to the Psalms direct the reader constantly to the wrong verse, namely, that of the Latin Vulgate from which they were first derived, not to that of the English Bible on whose pages they stand.

4. The claim made on the title page to be "newly translated" is, strictly speaking, inaccurate and contrary to the declaration of the translators in their preface.

ulary, Tyndale deserves the greatest credit; for the melody and harmony, Coverdale;[5] for scholarship and accuracy, the Geneva version.

The merits are not the same in all the books. From the division of the work among six independent panels, there arose naturally a considerable inequality in the execution. In the Old Testament, the historical books are translated better than the prophetical books, which present greater difficulties. The Book of Job is the most defective and is in several places unintelligible. The rendering of Isaiah, especially in the earlier portions, contains many errors and obscurities. The version of the Psalms is, upon the whole, less musical and rhythmical, though much more accurate, than Coverdale's, which held its place in the Book of Common Prayer until 1926. In the New Testament, the Gospels and Acts and even the Apocalypse are far better done than the Epistles,[6] notably Romans and Corinthians, which abound in minor inaccuracies.

In assessing the strengths and the weaknesses of the King James Version, one must acknowledge that the final product was certainly the best English Bible that had thus far been produced. Its English style is widely recognized as superb. The whole task of translation could hardly be better described than in Miles Smith's terse statement of purpose, "to deliver God's book unto God's people in a tongue which they could understand." This talent for cutting through verbiage and saying what is meant with force and in the fewest possible words was exactly what was needed.

But the work of the king's translators had also its basic weaknesses, several of them a part of its inheritance. There was no standard edition of the Hebrew Masoretic text of the Old Testament. In the New Testament, the late and corrupt Greek text of Erasmus as popularized and slightly modified by Stephanus and Beza was necessarily used, since nothing better was available. Codex Alexandrinus, the very existence of which was unsuspected by the translators, was not to arrive in England for a score of years; Codex

---

5. For example, the universally known phrase, "three score years and ten" is an English expression introduced by Coverdale in Psalm 90:10, where the Hebrew has plain "seventy."

6. For example, Hebrews 10:23 contains a curious mistake that is still perpetuated in modern printings of the KJV, where the Greek word *elpis*, which means "hope," is wrongly rendered "faith."

Vaticanus, though reported in the Vatican catalog of 1481, would for several centuries remain inaccessible to Protestant scholars; and Codex Sinaiticus, its value unrecognized, lay undisturbed at St. Catharine's monastery awaiting rescue from flames and oblivion by Tischendorf in the middle of the nineteenth century.

The first printing of the version, as would be expected, contained some typographic errors—averaging about one in ten pages. In Exodus 14:10, three whole lines were repeated: "the children of Israel lift up their eyes, and beholde, the Egyptians marched after them, and they were sore afraid." A printer's error that has been perpetuated in editions of the KJV to the present time is "strain at a gnat" (Matt. 23:24) instead of "strain out a gnat." Of all the misprints that have disfigured various printings of the version, none has been so scandalous as the omission of the word "not" from the seventh commandment in an edition of 1631, which then read "Thou shalt commit adultery" (Exod. 20:14), for which the king's printers were fined three hundred pounds by Archbishop Laud.

Notable for careful editorial work in the interest of obtaining an "authentique corrected Bible" were the Cambridge editions of 1629 and 1638. Still more comprehensive corrections and amendments were made by Dr. Thomas Paris, Cambridge, 1762, and by Dr. Benjamin Blayney, Oxford, 1769. Most of Paris's edition was destroyed by fire, and so it had little influence.

With the publication of the King James Version, the history of the English Bible closes for many a long year. Partly, no doubt, this was due to the troubled times that came upon England in that generation and the next. When the constitutions of church and state alike were being cast into the melting pot, there was little time for detailed discussion as to the exact text of the Scriptures and little peace for the labors of scholarship. But the main reason for this pause in the work was that, for the moment, finality had been reached. The version of 1611 was an adequate translation of the Greek and Hebrew texts as they were then known to scholars, and the common people eventually came to find that its language appealed to them with a greater charm and dignity than that of the Genevan version to which they had been accustomed.

A few attempts were made later in the seventeenth century to revise the King James Version or even to produce a fresh translation, but nothing came of them. The Long Parliament seriously thought of a new revision. A bill was introduced in April 1653 to the effect that a committee be appointed to revise King James's Version, but the project failed because of the dissolution of the Parliament in 1660.

As time passed, expressions of dissatisfaction with the King James Bible began to be replaced by the growth of approval for the version. From the 1760s onward, critical evaluation became increasingly favorable, and the 1611 version quietly superseded all its predecessors and rivals in the family and in the church. It owes its authority and popularity not to royal favor or legal enactments, but—what is far better—to its intrinsic merits and the verdict of English readers in general.[7]

In the nineteenth century, the board of managers of the American Bible Society expressed concern that their English Bibles be correctly printed. In 1847 the board charged a committee to investigate the matter and prepare a standard text for the society. The committee's report pointed out that although there were twenty-four thousand variations among the half-dozen copies obtained from well-known printers, "there is not one, which mars the integrity of the text, or affects any doctrine or precept of the Bible." After lengthy discussions, in 1861 various kinds of changes (chiefly orthographic) were introduced into the society's editions of the King James Bible. Further changes were made in 1932 to conform the orthography to American usage, and pronunciation marks were placed over most proper names. No further changes were made until the Reference Bible of 1962, in which the text was arranged in paragraph form, section headings were inserted, pronunciation marks simplified, a few changes in punctuation and orthography introduced, and a new system of references prepared.[8]

The most recent effort made by a Bible publisher to modernize the language of the King James Bible was undertaken in the last third of the twentieth century by the Thomas Nelson Corporation, Nashville, Tennessee. The New Testament of the New King James

7. See David Norton, *A History of the Bible as Literature*, vol. 2, *From 1700 to the Present Day* (Cambridge: Cambridge University Press, 1993).

8. For further details, see A. S. Herbert, *Historical Catalogue of Printed Editions of the English Bible, 1525–1961* (London: British and Foreign Bible Society; New York: American Bible Society, 1968), pp. 397–99.

Version was issued in 1979 and the entire Bible in 1982, the work
of "119 scholars, editors and church leaders" (so the dust jacket
states).

In older editions of the King James Version, the frequency of
the connective *and* far exceeded the limits of present-day English
usage. Biblical linguists agree that the Hebrew and Greek original
words for this conjunction may commonly be translated otherwise, depending on the immediate context. Therefore, the Nelson
NKJV frequently replaces *and* with alternatives such as *but, however,
now, so, then,* and *thus,* when the original language permits.

Contrary to the style of the 1611 Bible (as well as unsupported
by the biblical manuscripts), pronouns referring to God, Jesus
Christ, and the Holy Spirit are capitalized. Where the word *Lord*
occurs in a New Testament quotation from an Old Testament passage that contains "the covenant name of God" (p. iv), the New
Testament passage prints the word using capital letters (LORD).

In evaluating the NKJV, one is struck here and there by the continued presence of Elizabethan style and expressions, such as "day
of his espousals" (Song of S. 3:11), "dandled" (Isa. 66:12), "hew
down trees" (Jer. 6:6), and "purge the threshing floor" (Matt.
3:12). Much more serious is the continued reliance on an inferior
edition of the Greek text (see pp. 77–78 above), even where it involves a totally spurious passage (1 John 5:7).

—

five

Between the King James Bible and the Revised Version

People often suppose that when the story of the making of the English Bible had reached its culminating point in the publication of the King James or Authorized Version of 1611, it remained at a standstill until work began in 1870 on the Revised Version. The fact is, however, that several English translations appeared in both Britain and North America during the eighteenth and nineteenth centuries. Most of these private versions, as they may be called, are often passed over in complete silence by historians of the English Bible and are a forgotten chapter in its history. The following are among the more noteworthy examples of such translations.

Edward Harwood's New Testament (1768)

A century after the publication of the King James Version and the general acceptance it attained in succeeding generations, its

position was challenged by a classical scholar and biblical critic
named Edward Harwood. Dissatisfied with what he termed "the
bald and barbarous language of the old vulgar version," in 1768
Harwood issued a rendering of the New Testament[1] in the elevated style of English that was current among many British authors in the second half of the eighteenth century.

In the preface (p. iii), Dr. Harwood asks the readers to bear in
mind that "this is not a *verbal* translation, but a *liberal* and *diffusive*
version of the sacred classics, and is calculated to answer the purpose of an explanatory paraphrase as well as a free and elegant
translation." He states (p. v) his belief that

> *such* a Translation of the New Testament might induce persons of a
> liberal education and polite state to peruse the sacred volume, and
> that such a version might prove of signal service to the cause of
> truth, liberty, and Christianity, if men of cultivated and improved
> minds, especially YOUTH, could be allured by the innocent strata-
> gem of a *modern style,* to read a book, which is now, alas! too gener-
> ally neglected and disregarded by the young and gay, as a volume
> containing little to amuse and delight.

Harwood's translation is what one would expect from the expansive, condescending style of the preface. He aimed at elegance, per-
spicuity, and propriety, and achieved pomposity. Typical of his rendering is the translation of Peter's words at the Transfiguration of
Jesus: "Oh, Sir! what a delectable residence we might establish here!"

The simple and chaste language of Mary's *Magnificat* in the King
James Version (Luke 1:46–48) is transposed by Harwood so as to
read:

> My soul with reverence adores my Creator! and all my faculties
> with transport join in celebrating the goodness of God, my saviour,

1. The title page reads: *A Liberal Translation of the New Testament; being an
Attempt to translate the Sacred Writings with the same Freedom, Spirit, and Elegance,
with which other English Translations from the Greek Classics have lately been executed:
The Design and Scope of each Author being strictly and impartially explored, the True Significance and Force of the Original critically observed, and, as much as possible, transfused
into our Language, and the Whole elucidated and explained upon a new and rational
Plan: With Select Notes, Critical and Explanatory.* By E. Harwood. Volume 1, Gospels
and Acts; volume 2, Romans–Revelation, followed by Clement's *Epistle to the
Corinthians* (London, 1768).

who hath in so signal a manner condescended to regard my obscure and humble station—Transcendent goodness! every future age will now conjoin in celebrating my distinguished happiness!

The *Nunc Dimittis* of the aged Simeon (Luke 2:29–32) is as follows:

O God, thy promise to me is amply fulfilled!—I now quit the port of human life with satisfaction and joy! since thou hast indulged mine eyes with so divine a spectacle, as the great Messiah! Whom thou hast now sent into the world to bless mankind—to impart happiness to *Israel*, and to diffuse sacred light among the benighted *Heathens*!

The opening sentences of the parable of the Prodigal Son (Luke 15:11–12) are an example of the contrived and artificial style imposed on the simple and direct language of the Gospel:

A GENTLEMAN of a splendid family and opulent fortune had two sons. One day the younger approached his father, and begged him in the most importunate and soothing terms to make a partition of his effects betwixt himself and his elder brother—The indulgent father, overcome by these blandishments, immediately divided all his fortunes betwixt them.

Today Harwood's rendering into the idiom of Hume and Johnson is a literary curio. It was bound to have a very temporary and limited appeal—to be forgotten except when someone disinters it "to point a moral or adorn a tale." The moral is that we can learn from it the folly of what Archbishop Trench called "the worship of the fleeting present, of the transient fashions of the hour in language, with contempt of that stable past which in all likelihood will be the enduring future, long after these fashions have passed away and are forgotten."

Charles Thomson's Bible (1808)

The honor of producing the first translation of the Scriptures in English made and published in America belongs to Charles Thomson, the third of six children of John Thomson, a Scots-Irish Presbyterian of northern Ireland. In 1739, shortly after the death of his mother, Charles emigrated with his father and two or three of his brothers to America. John Thomson became ill on the voyage and died within sight of the coast. The ship's captain disposed of the body in the sea to save the expense of a land burial, and having confiscated most of the children's patrimony, he set them ashore at Lewes at the Cape of Delaware. Charles, a ten-year-old impoverished orphan, was placed in the care of a local blacksmith, an acquaintance of the ship's master.

One night the lad overheard that the smith was planning to have him indentured as an apprentice. But he had higher aspirations than the forge and escaped by running away. On the road, a kindhearted woman of a local family offered him a seat in her carriage. During their conversation together, she asked him what he wanted to be. The precocious reply that he wanted to be a scholar so pleased her that she took him home and put him in school. About 1743, through the generosity of several benefactors, he entered the Reverend Francis Alison's academy at New London, Chester County, Pennsylvania. After gaining a solid grounding in the classics from Alison, a graduate of Edinburgh University, in the late 1740s Thomson opened a school of his own on the farm of John Chambers in New Castle County, Delaware.

At the end of 1750, Thomson moved to Philadelphia where he became a tutor in Latin and Greek at the new Philadelphia Academy, established by Benjamin Franklin and which later became the University of Pennsylvania. With Franklin's aid, Thomson devoted himself to some areas of study that had been neglected earlier.

In September 1755, Thomson became head tutor of Latin at the Friends' Public School in Philadelphia. Through this position, he came to the attention of the Quakers' "Friendly Association," which enlisted him in support of opposing the Indian policy being pursued by the colony's proprietors. To this end, Thomson was chosen to serve as secretary for the Delaware Indians in their meetings with colonial officials. He so won the confidence of the Indians that he was adopted into their tribe and given the name "The Man Who Speaks the Truth." In the course of his duties, Thomson examined all of the acts of the assembly and their treaties with the Indians and published a report that was highly critical of Pennsylvania's proprietors.

In 1760 Thomson abandoned teaching for a series of business ventures. He first established a Philadelphia dry goods business, which did not prosper. He next turned briefly to rum distilling but moved, in 1770, to New Jersey as the business manager of an iron-works of which he was part owner. By the autumn of 1772, he had returned to Philadelphia and the following year was a leader of resistance to the landing of the East India Company tea, writing incendiary handbills in support of the patriot position.

Thereafter, he was increasingly, and finally totally, engrossed by politics. In the events preceding the American Revolution, Thomson played a large and influential role. Unanimously chosen as secretary of the Continental Congress, for nearly fifteen years he sat at the secretarial table and listened to the debates, minuting the birth-records of a nation. Thomson's last official act as secretary of Congress was to make a seven-day journey as messenger of the Congress, then sitting in New York, to Mount Vernon in Virginia, in order to notify George Washington of his election to the presidency of the United States and to accompany the new president to his inauguration at New York. Thomson had hoped for a significant post in the new government, but none was offered him.

By late summer of 1789, Thomson was reconciled to the fact that he would never again hold public office; he sent a letter of resignation to President Washington and received in reply a handsome acknowledgment of his services. In his sorrow and bitterness, he withdrew to his wife's country estate at Harriton—from her maiden name, Harrison—near Bryn Mawr, to live another thirty-five years. Henceforth a gentleman-farmer, far from taking his well-earned ease, he devoted his time to revising and perfecting a version of the Scriptures that he hoped would answer concerns about the authenticity of Jesus' claims and the Bible's credibility.

Thomson had been aware that when the New Testament writers quoted from the Old Testament, they almost always used the Septuagint version. Being shocked to learn that no English translation of the Septuagint was in existence, he was determined to make such a rendering from John Field's 1665 Cambridge edition of the Greek text. Field's publication was descended from the Sixtine edition (1587) based on the fourth-century Codex Vaticanus, at that time the earliest known manuscript of the Septuagint. His edition, however, was a so-called Puritan Septuagint, which included only the books approved for the Old Testament by the Westminster Confession of 1643–48, and which omitted the non-canonical Apocrypha and the hymns in the third chapter of Daniel. In Thomson's translation, the books were arranged according to the order of the King James Bible with two short additions: the 151st Psalm and a supplement following the close of the Book of Job, giving Job's ancestry.

For the New Testament, it has not been ascertained which edition of the Greek text Thomson utilized. In any case, it can only have been some uncritical copy of the so-called Textus Receptus (Received Text) with meager indications of variant readings. Departures from the Textus Receptus have been noticed at Matthew 6:13; Acts 9:20; 11:20; 1 Corinthians 9:22; 1 Peter 3:15; and 1 John 5:7–8, the last a place where the Received Text had been in error since Erasmus's third edition.

Thomson published his translation of the Old and New Testaments at Philadelphia in 1808–9. The printer, Jane Aitken, was one of the very few woman printers in America and certainly the first woman to print any part of the Scriptures. She produced one thousand copies of a beautifully crafted four-volume set, the Old Testament in three volumes and the New in the fourth (each measuring five by eight inches).

Though Thomson's translation is favorably regarded by biblical scholars today, at the time of its publication, the average reader little comprehended its worth, and it never enjoyed wide popular appeal. Consequently, it had only a limited sale and was not financially successful. Many of the unsold copies were eventually disposed of as waste paper.

To occupy his time after the death of his wife, Hannah, in 1807, Thomson turned once again to biblical studies. Even while the Bible was in the process of printing, he had begun to draw up a harmony of the four Evangelists from his translation, following generally the order of Philip Doddridge's harmony. Thomson believed that by arranging the facts presented in the Gospels, setting them in parallel columns, he had "removed the seeming inconsistencies with which they are charged and shown that instead of contradicting, they strengthen and confirm one another's narrative." After several years of searching for a publisher, in 1815 he issued at his own expense one thousand copies of *A Synopsis of the Four Evangelists; or, A regular history of the conception, birth, doctrine, mira-*

cles, death, resurrection, and ascension of Jesus Christ, in the words of the Evangelists (Philadelphia: published for the author by William Mc-Culloch, printer, 1815). The volume closes with thirty pages of "Notes, critical and explanatory," in which Thomson provides seventy-six longer or shorter notes keyed to specific sections of the synopsis.

It is appropriate now to present some specimens of Thomson's rendering of the biblical text. In his notebook, which deals with some of the problems and intricacies of translating, he indicated the standards he had set for his work:

> To translate well is: 1, to give a just representation of the purpose of an author; 2, to convey into the translation the author's spirit and manner; 3, to give it a quality of an original by making it appear natural, a natural copy without applying the words improperly, or in a meaning not warranted by use, or combining them in such a way which renders the sense obscure, and the construction ungrammatical or harsh.

Thomson's rendering of the Greek text of the Old Testament does not, of course, differ greatly from that of the King James Version made from the Hebrew text, but the differences are meaningful. Often the changes in wording reflect changes in language that had taken place in the United States. The language in use in King James's England was no longer the language of Americans in the nineteenth century. Thomson realized this, and he devoted a great amount of time to his task (making at least four complete manuscript copies of the entire Bible) in order to insure that his rendering used the language of the people. The style is sparse and easy-to-read nineteenth-century English. The New Testament is perhaps more polished than the Old Testament, but both make interesting reading. Some familiar passages as rendered by Thomson illustrate the language and the soundness of his rendering.

> The Lord is my shepherd. I shall want nothing. In a verdant pasture he hath fixed my abode. He hath fed me by gently flowing water and restored my soul. He hath led me in paths of righteousness for his name's sake. For though I walk amidst the shades of death: I will fear no ills, because thou art with me; thy rod and thy staff have been my comfort. Thou hast spread a table before me; in the presence of them who afflict me. With oil thou hast anointed my head;

and thine exhilarating cup is the very best. Thy mercy will surely follow me all the days of my life; and my dwelling shall be in the house of the Lord to length of days. (Psalm 23)

When David was old—far advanced in years, they covered him with clothes, but he was not warmed; therefore his servants said, Let a young virgin be sought out for the king, that she may attend him, and chafe him, and lie in his bosom, that my lord the king may be warmed. So they sought for a beautiful virgin, through all the borders of Israel, and having found Abisag, the Somanite, they brought her to the king. The young woman was indeed very beautiful, and she chafed the king, and waited on him, but the king knew her not. (3 Kings [the LXX designation for 1 Kings] 1:1–4)

After Psalm 150, Thomson has the following note and the supplementary psalm:

> N. B. There is in the Septuagint another Psalm, with this title:—This Psalm on David was written by himself in prose, when he fought in single combat with Goliath. I was little among my brethren, and the youngest of my father's family. I fed my brother's flocks. My hand had made an organ; and my fingers had tuned a psaltery. But who will tell my Lord. My Lord himself heareth. He sent his messenger and took me from my father's flocks and anointed me with anointing oil. My brothers were comely and great; but the Lord did not delight in them. I went out to meet the Philistine, and he cursed me by his idols. But I drew my own sword and cut off his head, and took away reproach from the children of Israel.

In the New Testament, probably the first thing that strikes the reader of Thomson's version is the relative rarity of certain theological terms. According to the analysis made by Kendrick Grobel,[2] "gospel" occurs only thirteen times; the usual rendering of *euangelion* is "glad tidings" (57 times); "good news" occurs five times, "message of peace" once. *Euangelizō* is never "preach" but usually "proclaim" (34) or "publish" (12). For *repent* and *repentance,* he prefers "reform" and "reformation," also using "change of mind" (3). *Temptation* usually becomes "trial." In Romans, "grace" occurs only once, "favour" 22 times. In the Gospels, *pistis* is predominately

---

2. Kendrick Grobel, "Charles Thomson, First American N.T. Translator—An Appraisal," *Journal of Bible and Religion* 11 (1943): 145–51.

"faith," but in Romans, the more intellectual word "belief" predominates over "faith" two to one; four times the gerund "believing" is effectively used. "Church" occurs only once (Matt. 16:18); otherwise *ekklēsia* is "congregation" (once "assembly," Acts 19:38). *Makarios* is nearly always "happy"; "blessed" only with attributes of the Trinity. "In all this," Grobel comments, "a certain accommodation to every-day speech is undeniable, but what is theological language, after all, but a specific use of every-day language?"[3]

In the thirteenth chapter of 1 Corinthians, Thomson used "love" instead of the King James's "charity," and in John 1:14, an interesting piece of imagery from the Greek is given by "Now the Word became incarnate, and dwelt as in a tent among us." Other passages might be given, but these show the language, the force, and the style of Thomson's translation. On the whole, the work of this solitary layman-translator, working without any of our present aids, succeeded in making in the infancy of American scholarship a clear and felicitous rendering of the New Testament that clarified and simplified the King James Version.

As was mentioned earlier, in its day Thomson's translation of the Septuagint attracted only limited interest and turned out to be a financial loss. In the twentieth century, however, his work was reprinted twice, once in Great Britain and once in the United States—and this despite the availability since 1844 of another English translation, that prepared by Sir Lancelot C. L. Brenton and issued in two volumes by S. Bagster and Sons in London. In the early part of the twentieth century, S. F. Pells issued in two volumes a photographic facsimile of Thomson's rendering of the Septuagint (London: Skeffington and Son, 1904).

Fifty years after Pells's verbatim reprint, C. A. Muses published a revised and slightly enlarged edition under the title *The Septuagint Bible: The Oldest Version of the Old Testament in the Translation of Charles Thomson* (Indian Hills, Colo.: Falcon's Wing, 1954). Muses included the additional material found in the Greek text of the Book of Esther, material that expands the canonical Hebrew text and therefore was omitted by Thomson. Furthermore, on the basis of Thomson's longhand corrections written in his own desk copy

3. Grobel, "Charles Thomson," p. 148.

of the printed work,[4] Muses incorporated selected addenda and corrigenda, but happily refused to introduce the wholesale change of "Lord" to "Jehovah." On the other hand, and contrary to most English renderings of the Bible, Muses thought it necessary to capitalize pronominal references to the Supreme Being.

Noah Webster's Bible (1833) = Webster's Dictionary

The American lexicographer and philologist, Noah Webster (1758–1843), was born at West Hartford, Connecticut, and attended Yale College, but was graduated in the middle of his course after serving as a volunteer in the Revolutionary War. He studied law and was admitted to the bar in 1781, but decided to teach school instead. In 1782, while teaching at Goshen, New York, he began to write his *Grammatical Institute of the English Language*. It was made up of a speller, a grammar, and a reader written for the use of schoolchildren. The first part, often revised, became his *Elementary Spelling Book*; this was very popular and had a wide sale for more than one hundred years. By 1850, when the total population was around 23 million, the annual sales of the spelling book were about one million, and the figures increased yearly, finally attaining a sale of more than 60 million copies.

Deriving his income from schoolbooks, Webster devoted himself to compiling a dictionary. In 1806 he brought out *A Compendious Dictionary of the English Language*, which was somewhat like an encyclopedia. Following the publication of the dictionary, he worked at another that would be more satisfactory to him. This, his greatest work, was the *American Dictionary of the English Language* (1828), which included twelve thousand words and forty thousand definitions that had never before appeared in any other dictionary. Its definitions were excellent, and its sales, reaching three hundred thousand annually, indicate that it may have helped to standardize American pronunciation. Webster com-

---

4. The copy is preserved in the oldest public library in America, The Library Company of Philadelphia, to which it was presented in 1825 by Charles Thomson's nephew, John Thomson.

In leafing through the volumes, the present writer observed that the corrections are written neatly with a pen and black ink. Some stand in the margin, others are over the word being canceled, and more lengthy corrections are written on strips of paper pasted over the line (or lines) being replaced.

pleted an enlarged edition in 1840, and the dictionary has since been revised many times. After his death, his heirs sold the rights to the dictionary to the G. and C. Merriam Company of Springfield, Massachusetts.

Following the initial publication of his *American Dictionary* in 1828, Webster began to give serious attention to revising the King James Version of the Bible. Unlike Edward Harwood, Webster held that version in high regard. "Its language," he said, "is in general correct and perspicuous; the genuine popular English of Saxon origin; peculiarly adapted to the subjects, and in many passages, uniting sublimity to beautiful simplicity." But he called attention to the fact that

> in the lapse of two or three centuries changes have taken place, which, in particular passages, impair the beauty, in others, obscure the sense of the original languages. Some words have fallen into disuse; and the signification of others, in current popular use, is not the same now as it was when they were introduced into the version. . . . Whenever words are understood in a sense different from that of the original languages, they do not present the reader the *Word of God.* . . . A version of the scriptures for popular use should consist of words expressing the sense which is most common in popular usage, so that the *first ideas* suggested to the reader should be the true meaning of such words according to the original languages. . . . That many words in the present version fail to do this, is certain. My principal aim is to remedy this evil.

As would be expected from a dictionary maker, Webster began with an introduction in which he carefully listed and explained the alterations he had made in the English text of the King James Version. He found some 150 words and phrases to be erroneous or misleading, and these he corrected in the various passages where they appeared. He substituted "who" for "which," when it refers to persons; and "its" for "his," when it refers to things. He used "Be not anxious" for "Take no thought"; "food" for "meat"; "falsehood" for "leasing"; "button" for "tache"; "boiled" for "sodden"; "hinder" for the obsolete sense of "let" (as in 2 Thess. 2:7); and various words appropriate to the context for "prevent" in its obsolete sense of "go before" (as in Ps. 119:147; Matt. 17:25). He used the term "Holy Spirit" instead of "Holy Ghost." Where Paul wrote "would that," the King James Version makes him say "would to God," and in fourteen cases where he wrote "be it not so," the King James Version reads "God forbid"; Webster removed the insertion of reference to God from both these expressions. The occasional use of the singular number of the verb with a plural subject (e.g., Luke 5:10; 9:17) was corrected. He also standardized the usage of *shall* and *will*, *should* and *would*. In this part of the work, the "New England grammarian" did yeoman service, and the later Revised Version took over nearly every one of his changes, although no credit for his previous labors was given.

In addition to the kinds of changes mentioned above, Webster introduced another type of amendment in the language, which he considered of very grave importance. In his own words at the close of his introduction,

> To these may be added many words and phrases, very offensive to delicacy and even to decency. . . . Language which cannot be uttered in promiscuous [mixed] company without a violation of decorum, or the rules of good breeding, exposes the scriptures to the scoffs of unbelievers, impairs their authority, and multiplies or confirms the enemies of our holy religion.[5]

For a time Webster's amended edition was used in many Congregational churches; a second edition was published in 1841, and three editions of his revision of the New Testament were printed in 1838, 1840, and 1841.

But then his work faded from public view. It has only recently been resuscitated by Baker Book House, which published in 1987 a facsimile edition (in a deluxe binding) of the initial publication issued in New Haven in 1833.

Julia E. Smith's Bible (1876)

Julia Evelina Smith (1792–1878) was the first woman to translate the entire Bible into English. She was an unusual woman in

---

5. In the following passages, Webster introduced various euphemisms in place of the expressions used in the King James Version: Gen. 20:18; 29:31; 30:22; 34:30; 38:9, 24; Exod. 7:18; 16:24; Lev. 19:29; 21:7; Deut. 22:21; 23:1; 28:57; Judg. 2:17; 1 Sam. 1:5; 1 Kings 14:10; 16:11; 21:21; 2 Kings 9:8; 18:27; Job 3:10–12; 40:17; Ps. 22:9, 10; 38:5; 106:39; Eccles. 11:5; Isa. 36:12; Ezek. 16 and 23; John 11:39; Eph. 5:5.

an unusual family; she was the fourth of five daughters born to Zephaniah Holister Smith, a graduate of Yale College and successively a minister, a doctor, and a lawyer, and Hannah Hadassah Hickok, a linguist, astronomer, poet, and gentlewoman farmer. Because of their own intellectual bent, Hannah and Zephaniah considered a good education of great importance to their daughters. Their idea of a good education, however, differed in significant ways from that of most of their contemporaries. Education for women typically focused on increasing their social usefulness as wives and mothers; anything beyond the most rudimentary reading and ciphering, a little music, and needlework was seen as not only unnecessary but dangerous, for it would rob them of their charms and make them restive and domineering.

Hannah and Zephaniah Smith rejected this approach to educating women. To them, the best education for their daughters was identical to what they would have provided to sons, which meant heavy emphasis on the classics, history, mathematics, and languages. After elementary education, supplemented by wide reading at home, the eldest daughter, then thirteen years old, was sent to a boarding school at Norwich, Connecticut, a boys' academy that admitted girls. Later on, she and her sisters attended Litchfield Academy.

When they had surpassed the resources available in these schools, the Smiths were innovative in finding new avenues for education. For example, both Julia and her younger sister, Abby, spent at least one summer living with a French family in New Haven. The older sisters also took responsibility for teaching the younger sisters. For example, throughout 1813 when Abby was sixteen years old and Julia was twenty-one, Julia tutored Abby in Latin. Julia also taught Abby by example: in 1816 she decided to teach herself Greek, using the Greek grammar her father had brought her from Hartford.

For most of their lives, the two sisters lived with their parents and three older sisters at the family farm in Glastonbury, Connecticut. After Zephaniah died in 1836, Hannah and the five sisters managed the farm and continued to sell farm products in order to provide income. Money had been available from Zephaniah's law practice and the abundant sale of farm produce. The fact that the family was financially comfortable was ultimately to bring Julia and Abby into conflict with the Glastonbury authorities.

Roused to a deep and personal study of the Bible by the millennial messages of eschatological doom preached by William Miller, a Vermont farmer, the Smiths believed that he had discovered the key to Daniel's prophecies. Miller predicted that the end of the world was at hand and founded a sect of Adventists. The year 1843 was the date agreed upon for the second coming of Christ.

To heighten the sense of ominous expectation, a brilliant comet blazed across the sky in 1842, a sure precursor according to believers. At the end of 1842, Julia's diary is filled with references to Miller and his writings, which she and Abby had been studying daily. The last entry that year reads:

> Monday 31 [December 1842] I have stayed in the house all day except I have been walking in the afternoon to see Henry Welles.[6] I read the Bible almost all day. I've eaten nothing since yesterday noon. It is the last day of the year, perhaps all of us should be prepared to enter the new year 1843 which according to Mr. Miller could be the last year of this world.[7]

Miller had relied on the King James Version in working out his chronology. Since the world had not ended, but Miller's mathematics seemed to be correct, then perhaps the error was in the translation. Could it be that the true meaning of God's Word had been distorted by well-meaning but inept translators and interpreters? As Julia stated in the preface to her translation, she and her sisters

> saw by the margin [of the King James Version] that the text had not been given literally, and it was the literal meaning we were seeking.

6. Welles had grown up less than a quarter of a mile from the Smiths. He walked over there frequently to study French under Julia and stayed in touch with her until the end of her life. He reported in his *Autobiography and Reminiscences*, vol. 1 (Minneapolis, 1899) that after the Smiths had espoused the doctrines of Miller, they "renounced all human authority in religious doctrine, insisted on a hidden sense in the Bible which they could see but which they could not communicate, gave up everything that suggested a love for the world, turning the pictures to the wall, covering the piano with a pall, and putting the plants in the cellar."

7. Paradoxically, that is the last entry in her entire diary. After keeping it for thirty-two years in French, from this point onward she entered only meteorological data in English with an entry about the death of Laurilla, an older sister, on March 19, 1857.

I had studied Latin and Greek at school, and began by translating the Greek of the New Testament, and then the Septuagint, from which our Saviour quoted one or two texts which are not in the Hebrew Bible; and there is now said to be no Hebrew Bible extant so old as the Septuagint. We all had a strong desire to learn the significance of the proper names, and I wrote to a learned friend about it, and he advised me to study Hebrew saying "it was a simple language and easily learned, there being but one book in the world of pure Hebrew, which was the Bible."

So, at the age of fifty-five, Julia set about the task of learning Hebrew with the same single-mindedness she had earlier applied to Greek and Latin. According to one account, she would become so immersed in the process of translation that she often did not hear the dinner bell and had to be reminded by her sisters to eat.

Thus began eight years of concentrated effort (from 1847 to 1855) during which time she entered her translation of the Bible into small, hand-bound folios, which would eventually contain more than ten thousand single-spaced handwritten pages of translation. By 1855 she had translated the Bible five times, twice from the Greek (Septuagint and New Testament), twice from the Hebrew, and once from the Vulgate, each time striving to come nearer the original meaning.

Julia had not set about the task of translating with any intention of having her work published. The project was for her own personal satisfaction, and the published version of her Bible translation might never have become a reality had not Abby protested the double-billing and increase of the tax bills presented to her and Julia by the town of Glastonbury in 1869. When the sisters pressed the local tax office for more details, they learned that the town "fathers" had need of more money to pay the bills. As a solution, an arbitrary assessment had been made to increase the property tax on the Smith farm. Without any male family members to represent them, the sisters sounded the battle cry of one hundred years earlier and charged that they were victims of taxation without representation. Deaf to their complaints, the tax collector threatened to seize the Smith property, which then could be sold at auction to pay the taxes.

It became apparent that if the Smith sisters, now in their seventies, did not fight the injustice of taxation without representation, their entire life holdings might be seized while they remained legally helpless to stop the process. The sisters made use of an interested and sympathetic press and a newly emerging women's rights movement to fight their case. Most especially aggravating was the seizure of the sisters' seven prized Alderney cows, which not only provided food and income for them but a type of companionship as well. The press (not only local but throughout the country) made much of a farcical parade led by the tax collector, accompanied by four men with a dog and a drum, as they marched the cows to a neighbor's farm for auction, with the Smith sisters and local townspeople following behind!

The whole matter was contested in the courts for years. The first trial was decided in favor of the Smith sisters, the second trial (the collector's appeal) was decided against them,[8] and the third trial finally found in their favor. No tax bill was ever paid on the Glastonbury property until 1879, when Julia married and the husband paid the bill rather than be taken to jail as the party responsible for his wife's debts.

While the legal case worked its way through the courts, the sisters decided to remove Julia's Bible translation manuscript from obscurity and to publish it to prove women's intellectual capabilities. Julia edited and redacted thousands of pages of translation, and the sisters contracted with the American Publishing Company of Hartford, Connecticut, to issue *The Holy Bible: Containing the Old and New Testaments; Translated Literally from the Original Tongues.* This was published in 1876 at their own expense, which amounted to four thousand dollars. One thousand copies were printed, containing eleven hundred pages each. The motivation was not to make money on the project (copies sold for $2.50), but rather partially to defray their tax bills (which were growing ever larger) and primarily to prove that "a woman can do more than any man has ever done," in translating single-handedly the entire Bible from Hebrew, Greek, and Latin.

Julia and Abby Smith undertook their publishing venture in order to prove a point, not to make a profit. The stress of the three trials necessary to establish that the Smith sisters had been wrong-

---

8. In 1877 Julia published at Hartford a booklet entitled *Abby Smith and her Cows, with the Report of the Law Case Decided Contrary to Law.*

fully treated by the town of Glastonbury took its toll and may have hastened Abby's death.

The books of the Old Testament in Smith's Bible are arranged in the order that they appear in Hebrew canon, with Chronicles at the end. Her translation is very literal, adhering closely to Hebrew and Greek idioms, and often makes quite unnatural English. She was guided by the notion that a given Hebrew or Greek word should always be represented by one and the same English word. The result, however, of such a policy of mechanical translation was much nonsense and in some passages almost complete mistranslation. The extent of the obscurity is suggested by Jeremiah 22:23, presented as a complete sentence and reading "Thou dwelling in Lebanon, building a nest in the cedars, how being compassionated in pangs coming to thee the pain as of her bringing forth."

Julia Smith had a very odd notion about Hebrew tenses. She writes in the preface, "It seems that the original Hebrews had no regard to time, and that the Bible speaks for all ages. . . . I think that the promiscuous use of tenses shows that there is something hidden, that we must search out." Paying no attention to the function of the Hebrew *waw* consecutive, in historical narratives she frequently translated the imperfect by the English future and the perfect by the English simple past. In the narrative of Genesis 1:26–28, Smith begins with the future tense, continues in verse 27 with the past tense, but reverts to the future in verse 28:

> 26. And God will say, We will make man in our image according to our likeness. . . . 27. And God will form man in his image, in the image of God he formed him: male and female he formed them. 28. And God will praise them, and God will say to them, be fruitful and multiply. . . .

In Genesis 3:13 the first woman says: "The serpent deceived me and I shall eat."

Isaiah 6:1 reads: "In the year King Uzziah died, and I shall see Jehovah sitting upon his throne. . . ."

Jonah 1:5 reads: "And Jonah went down to the sides of the ship, and he will lie down and snore."

Several other samples will give the reader an idea of Smith's style.

Psalm 17:8: "Watch me as the pupil of the daughter of the eye: thou wilt hide me in the shadow of thy wings."

Proverbs 15:17: "Good a ration of herbs and love there, above an ox of the stall and hatred with it."

Perhaps Julia Smith's initial mistake was to seek no help or advice for her venture, as she naïvely declares in the preface:

> It may be thought by the public in general that I have great confidence in myself, in not conferring with the learned in so great a work, but as there is but one book in the Hebrew tongue, and I have defined it word for word, I do not see that anybody can know more about it than I do.

It is not clear which Greek text of the New Testament Smith used. Matthew 5:22 omits "without cause," but "openly" remains in Matthew 6:4, 6, 18, as well as the doxology to the Lord's Prayer in 6:13. In 1 John 5:7–8 the "three heavenly witnesses" passage is enclosed within parentheses.

Angel is translated "messenger"; "immerse/immersion" are used instead of *baptize/baptism*; "the sent" appears for *apostles*, and the Greek verb *aphiēmi* is translated "let go," even in passages like the Lord's Prayer, where it means "forgive": "And let go to us our debts, as we let go to our debtors" (Matt. 6:12).[9]

---

9. The saga of the Julia E. Smith Bible has been told most fully in two recently published books: Kathleen L. Housley, *The Letter Kills but the Spirit Gives Life: The Smiths—Abolitionists, Suffragists, Bible Translators* (Glastonbury, Conn.: Historical Society of Glastonbury, 1993); and Susan J. Shaw, *A Religious History of Julia Evelina Smith's 1876 Translation of the Holy Bible: Doing More Than Any Man Has Ever Done* (San Francisco: Mellen Research University Press, 1993).

six

The British Revised Version (1881–85) and the American Standard Version (1901)

During the eighteenth and nineteenth centuries, increasing numbers of private English translations of the Bible were produced in Britain and in America. In addition, twenty-seven more or less different versions of only the New Testament were published by individuals. As time went on, however, the need was increasingly felt for a thorough revision of the 1611 Bible prepared by a committee of scholars representing diverse ecclesiastical affiliations.

The basic factor for any translation of the New Testament is, of course, the Greek text. By the middle of the nineteenth century, the study of the Greek manuscripts had shown beyond question that the King James Version was based upon a Greek text that

contained the accumulated errors of fifteen centuries of manuscript copying. It was essentially the Greek text as edited by Beza,
who closely followed the text issued by Erasmus, which had been
based on a mere handful of late medieval manuscripts.

In 1627, only sixteen years after the publication of the King
James Version, a priceless manuscript of the Bible, the Codex Alexandrinus, written in the fifth century, came to England, a gift to
the king from the patriarch of Constantinople. This greatly stimulated interest in the search for other ancient manuscripts of the Bible and in the collation of their various readings.

In 1830, a fresh period began, as scholars undertook the sifting
of textual evidence and the formulation of principles of textual
criticism in an attempt to recover the original Greek text as free as
possible from errors and additions. Then came the epoch-making
work of Constantine Tischendorf, discoverer of the Codex Sinaiticus and editor of the Codex Vaticanus, both dating from the fourth
century. These and other finds enabled the Cambridge University
scholars B. F. Westcott and F. J. A. Hort, after twenty-eight years
of joint labor, to come closer to the original text of the New
Testament.[1]

From the middle of the nineteenth century, proposals for the revision of the King James Version in keeping with the new knowledge of the Greek text were both advocated and opposed. In 1870
the introduction of a motion in the Upper House of the Convocation
of Canterbury resulted in the appointment of Old Testament and
New Testament companies of revisers, to which non-Anglican
scholars were co-opted. Just as the Bishops' Bible had been the basis
for the 1611 work, so now the King James Version was to be the
starting point. The revisers were instructed to "introduce as few alterations as possible into the Text of the Authorised Version consistently with faithfulness" and "to limit, as far as possible, the expression
of such alterations to the language of the Authorised and earlier English Versions."[2] No change was to be finally approved except by a
two-thirds majority; changes supported by only a simple majority
were to be noted in the margin.

1. For an account of these and other textual studies, see my *Text of the New
Testament: Its Transmission, Corruption, and Restoration*, 3d ed. (New York and
Oxford: Oxford University Press, 1992).
2. From the revisers' preface.

On July 7, 1870, the Lower House of Convocation passed a resolution requesting the Upper House to instruct the revision committee to invite the cooperation of American divines. This suggestion was accepted and acted on, though time passed before the actual cooperation could begin. It was arranged that Dr. Philip Schaff at Union Theological Seminary should select and invite suitable American scholars for the purpose. By December the arrangements for selection of the committee members was reported to be complete, but for one reason or another the group did not begin its active work until October 4, 1872.

Westcott and Hort were members of the British New Testament Company, and confidential advance copies of the Greek text they were editing were printed for the use of the revisers in England and America. Although both Westcott and Hort undoubtedly exercised very great influence on the judgment of the British company of revisers, they did not by any means control it, and a more traditional estimate of the evidence was usually defended by Dr. F. H. A. Scrivener.

During the years of work on the revision, the British proposals on successive sections of the Bible were sent to America, then returned with suggestions made by the appropriate American committee. A second revision was sent for the same treatment; then a third revision was made in England. Suggestions made by the Americans had to gain approval of two-thirds of the British committee in order to be accepted.

The agreement between the American and the British committees was as follows:

> If any differences shall still remain, the American Committee will yield its preferences for the sake of harmony; provided that such differences of reading and rendering as the American Committee may represent to the English Companies to be of special importance, be distinctly stated either in the Preface to the Revised Version, or in any Appendix to the volume, during a term of fourteen years from the date of publication, unless the American Churches shall sooner pronounce a deliberate opinion upon the Revised Version with the view of its being taken for public use.[3]

3. Quoted by Luther A. Weigle, *The English New Testament, from Tyndale to the Revised Standard Version* (New York: Abingdon-Cokesbury, 1949), p. 97.

In accordance with this agreement, the American committee prepared an appendix containing by no means a complete list of their rejected recommendations, but a minimum list of about three hundred that they considered to be of sufficient importance to record, in the hope that they might ultimately be incorporated into the text.

The task of revision took twice as long as it had taken to produce the 1611 Bible.[4] The New Testament, being shorter, was finished first and published on May 17, 1881, by the presses of Oxford and Cambridge Universities, which received exclusive copyright in return for the twenty thousand pounds they had advanced. The revisers themselves received no remuneration. Response was enthusiastic. In a few days, two million copies were sold in Britain, and in Philadelphia another 110,000. Two Chicago newspapers printed the entire New Testament in their issues of May 22.

The Old Testament appeared, with less demonstration, as a part of the whole Bible on May 19, 1885. To complete the project, the universities commissioned a revision of the Apocrypha, which appeared in 1895, a decided improvement on the King James Version of the Apocrypha. Altogether, a quarter century of work (1870–95) went into this English Revised Version, which, as a church-ordained revision of the 1611 Bible, can be called the fourth Authorized Version in English, succeeding those of 1539, 1568, and 1611.

After the publication of the English Revised Version of the Old Testament in 1885, the British committee disbanded, but the American committee decided to continue its organization so as to take such action as should be called for at the expiration of the fourteen-year period.

In the meantime, in 1881 and 1882, unauthorized editions of the Revised Version of the New Testament were published in New York and Philadelphia, which incorporated those of the readings preferred by the American committee that had been recorded in the appendix. In 1898 the Oxford and Cambridge University Presses published a similar edition for the American market, with a preface referring to it as the American Revised Bible. These edi-

---

4. The KJV took seven years to produce, from the Hampton Court Conference in 1604 to 1611. Work on the RV went on for fifteen years, from 1870 to 1885.

tions were unacceptable to the American committee, since they contained only the preferences recorded in the appendix, which had been purposely reduced in number.

Accordingly, in 1901, the American committee issued the American Standard Version of the Bible. This was a newly edited form of the Revised Version of 1881 and 1885, incorporating about six hundred readings and renderings preferred by the Americans. It was called the "Standard" edition because it had to compete with at least three editions that had been mechanically put together by others and then usurped the name of "American Version" or "American Revised Bible." Understandably, the American Standard Version was copyrighted to insure purity of text.

The American Standard Version substituted the name Jehovah for Lord and God wherever *YHWH* (the Tetragrammaton) occurs in the Hebrew text and used Holy Spirit for Holy Ghost. It also substituted "Sheol" for "the grave," "the pit," and "hell" in places where these terms had been retained from the 1611 Bible. In the New Testament, where earlier Greek manuscripts have been followed, the titles of the Gospels do not include "Saint," and the title of the Epistle to the Hebrews no longer attributes it to Paul the Apostle.

The American Standard Version also increased the number of changes made for the sake of euphemism. It was not possible in every case to find an appropriate substitute for terms that in modern times have become offensive, but when it seemed possible, the American revisers made a change. For example, the word "bowels" was tolerable when used in the literal sense but seemed offensive when employed in a psychological sense. Thus, no other word would be appropriate in 2 Samuel 20:10, but to retain that term in Jeremiah 4:19 or Lamentations 1:20 (as the English revisers had done) seemed both unpleasant and incorrect.

In English style the American revision introduced some distinct improvements over the British Revised Version. Archaic sixteenth-century words, like "bewray," "holpen," and "sith," were dropped, and "who" or "that" was used instead of "which" when relating to persons. The orthography of proper names was also vastly improved. The American committee omitted "for" before infinitives and changed "an" to "a" before "h" aspirated. (The latter change had been made in the British revision of the New Testament but not in that of the Old.) In Genesis 22:23, for the sake of clarity, the Americans preferred to retain the wording of the 1611 Bible ("these eight Milcah did bear to Nahor") rather than adopt the preference of the British "these eight did Milkah bear to Nahor" (which the British declared no hearer would mistake as meaning "milk a bear"!).

The fate of the Revised Version in Great Britain was disappointing. Complaints about its English style began to be made as soon as it appeared. Charles Hadden Spurgeon, the great English preacher at the close of the nineteenth century, tersely remarked that the Revised New Testament was "strong in Greek, weak in English." The revisers were often woodenly literal, inverting the natural order of words in English in order to represent the Greek order, and they carried the translation of the article and of the tenses beyond their legitimate limits. An example of the rather tortuous order is Luke 9:17, "And they did eat, and were all filled; and there was taken up that which remained over to them of broken pieces, twelve baskets."

Although these criticisms apply as well to the American Standard Version, in the United States the work of the revisers was somewhat more widely adopted than in Great Britain.[5] But in both countries the revision failed to supplant the King James Version in popular favor. Furthermore, proponents of other versions in a more modern idiom deprecated the revisers' continued use of archaic speech. Several of these are considered in the next chapter.

---

5. For subsequent modifications introduced into the American Standard Version, see pp. 149–51 below.

seven

Early Modern-Speech Versions

The publication of the Revised Version (1881–85) and the American Standard Version (1901), both of which offered a strictly formal rendering of the original texts, stimulated the production of modern-speech versions. From around the turn of the century, this movement was strengthened by the discoveries of large numbers of Greek papyri in Egypt. These papyri shed light on every aspect of the life of the Greek-speaking people of the ancient world. It became clear that the New Testament documents were written in a plain, simple style to meet the needs of ordinary men and women. Should they not then be translated into the same kind of English? This was the argument of translators of modern-speech versions.

Among modern-speech versions of the early twentieth century, several are of special significance because of the influence they exerted on the mid-century production of the Revised Standard Version. They are *The Twentieth Century New Testament,* Weymouth's *New Testament in Modern Speech,* Moffatt's *A New Translation of the Bible,* and Smith and Goodspeed's *The Bible: An American Translation.*

The Twentieth Century New Testament (1901; 1904)

At the beginning of the twentieth century, a modern English version of the New Testament was published on both sides of the Atlantic with the title *The Twentieth Century New Testament: A Translation into Modern English Made from the Original Greek (Westcott and Hort's Text).* The introduction stated that it was the work of a "company of about twenty persons, members of various sections of the Christian Church." The translation, which was published anonymously, began to appear in 1898, coming out in three parts. In 1901 the parts were issued in a single volume by Horace Marshall of London, and in America by the Fleming H. Revell Company. This was identified as a "Tentative Edition," and criticisms and suggestions were welcomed.

In 1904 appeared the "permanent edition," so called in a note, though on the title page it is called the "Revised Edition." There are differences between the two editions in almost every verse, usually in the direction of simpler diction. The changes are interesting and show the care bestowed by the translators on this work.

In 1933 the last survivor of the group of translators (so far as is known) deposited the secretary's records of their work in the John Rylands Library at Manchester. There, some twenty years later, they were consulted by Dr. Kenneth W. Clark, who published a fascinating account entitled "The Making of the Twentieth Century New Testament."[1] About half of the members of the committee were ministers of various churches, while others were lay people, but none of them belonged to the class of linguistic and textual experts who had produced the Revised Version of 1881–85. They did on occasion consult experts, but the real work was done by themselves. Their translating was moti-

---

1. Kenneth W. Clark, "The Making of the Twentieth Century New Testament," *Bulletin of the John Rylands University Library of Manchester* 38 (1955–56): 58–81.

vated by social causes and the desire to convey the Word of God in a plainer English idiom.

The committee had its origin in 1891 when Mrs. Mary Kingsland Higgs, the wife of a Congregational minister living at Oldham near Manchester, began to prepare an idiomatic translation of the Gospel of Mark for her children, who did not understand the language of the traditional English Bible. In another corner of England lived a signal and telegraph engineer, Ernest de Mérindol Malan of Newland, Hull. He was the grandson of a noted Swiss Reformed preacher (Dr. César Malan) and followed the custom of reading the Bible to his children. The family was bilingual, and Malan observed that the modern French version by Lasserre was better understood than was the traditional English.

As it happened, both Mrs. Higgs and Mr. Malan wrote to W. T. Stead, the editor of the *Review of Reviews,* expressing their desire for a modern English translation of the Scriptures. Stead referred the two correspondents to each other, and they soon began collaboration in translating the Gospel of Mark. As they progressed, they expanded the plan to include the four Gospels and the Book of Acts. To do this they sought to enlist additional partners, and Stead printed a notice in his journal asking for "co-workers in the task of translating the Gospels and the Acts of the Apostles into our every-day speech."

The first appeal for assistance brought together a strange assemblage of twenty persons. For a long time, they collaborated only by correspondence and never met. This had a fortunate result when, in 1892, Malan, as secretary of the project, requested each to provide an autobiographical sketch that would serve as an introduction to all the others. Fifteen of these sketches are preserved among the papers, and from them one can appreciate the diversity of backgrounds of the translators. The Reverend Henry Bazett described himself as a Huguenot ex-curate, though he had been ordained in the Church of England. Thomas Sibley Boulton, who was only twenty years old, had embraced socialism and wrote of his desire for "a reunion of Christianity." W. M. Copeland, who was a headmaster educated in Aberdeen, called himself "a Radical in Politics and Religion." W. M. Crook, the eldest son of an Irish Wesleyan minister, was a master in classics at Trinity College, Dublin. At twenty-one, ill health caused his temporary withdrawal. He later became a lecturer for the National

Liberal Club. The Reverend E. D. Girdlestone, at sixty-three, was possibly the oldest member and a stalwart associate who published a number of articles, mostly socialistic. A. Ingram was a Presbyterian, born in Aberdeen; he listed successive occupations as cowboy, grocer, draper, lawyer's and accountant's clerk, and journalist since 1880. He was a widower with three children. The Reverend E. Hampden-Cook, a Congregationalist and "broad Evangelical," had received his degree from Cambridge. In 1903 he prepared the posthumous Weymouth translation for publication (see the next section).

Besides Mrs. Higgs, the only other woman among the partners was Mrs. Sarah Elizabeth Butterworth Mee, who was related to Sir Joseph Butterworth, an emancipationist. She had married the Wesleyan minister Josiah Mee and taught a Sunday school class for twenty years. Mrs. Mee, and at least one other of the partners, knew no Greek, but they served on the English committee to review the translation for its proper idiom.

After the initial stages of the work, twelve more workers were enlisted. All together, thirty-five persons were associated with the translation. It was a company of liberal and independent thinkers, strong-minded and even opinionated. Their struggle with life—social, political, and intellectual—is reflected in the tensions and ill health they report, for hardly a single biography lacks this element. Clark comments:

> Certainly this company of translators is no ordinary assemblage, and it is difficult to imagine a more disparate group. The members range in age between 19 and 63. In education they vary widely. They represent all parts of the British Isles. About half of them are clergymen, of which probably none is a typical representative. Others are schoolmasters, business men, and housewives. . . . Among them, there are many whose records show a procession through successive religious affiliations. Several of the clergymen have experienced repeated doubts about their calling, and some have forsaken their orders altogether.[2]

In assessing the significance of *The Twentieth Century New Testament*, one must acknowledge that its great advantage was the

2. Clark, "The Making of the Twentieth Century New Testament," p. 65.

choice of a Greek text to translate. The Westcott and Hort text of 1881 was the best critical text that had yet appeared. In the translation, a modern format was achieved by arranging the text in a single column, and in paragraphs, while relegating chapter and verse numerals to the margin. Poetry was printed in its proper form, and Old Testament quotations were clearly set off from the main text.

In more than one passage, the translators clarified the meaning so admirably that later revisers adopted their rendering. For example, in Matthew 10:8 the familiar phrase, "Freely ye received, freely give" (KJV and RV), the adverbial phrase does not mean, as the English may suggest, generously or abundantly. The 1904 translators were quite correct in their version, "You have received free of cost, give free of cost," with which the NRSV agrees, "You have received without payment; give without payment."

In Matthew 26:27, the directive "Drink ye all of it" (KJV and RV) is ambiguous without punctuation, and many have mentally punctuated it as, "Drink ye, all of it." But the 1904 edition is clear and correct when it renders the equally clear Greek, "Drink from it, all of you."

In John 1:5, instead of the traditional "And the darkness comprehendeth it not" (KJV) or the RV alternative "apprehended it not," the 1904 translation rendered the sentence "And the darkness never overpowered it." This sense was both clear and correct and has been followed in the RSV, "And the darkness has not overcome it."

Another obscure verse the translators clarified was Acts 5:24. When the imprisoned apostles mysteriously disappeared, the leaders "doubted of them whereunto this would grow" (KJV). The RV did no better with the verse, but the 1904 edition made sense of it: "They were perplexed about the Apostles and as to what all this would lead to." All important translations since have resembled this phrasing.

First Corinthians 10:24 is indeed perplexing when Paul exhorts, "Let no man seek his own, but every man another's wealth" (KJV). The RV saw the need to correct this to ". . . but each his neighbour's good." But the 1904 edition really established the form for this verse. "A man must not study his own interests, but the interests of others." This pioneer phrasing has been followed closely by all the best translations.

In the Hymn of Love in 1 Corinthians 13, the 1904 edition again pioneered when it translated *agapē* as "love" rather than the traditional "charity." This rendering has been followed by virtually all Protestant translations since.

Many readers have been confused by Paul's advice in Philippians 4:6, "Be careful for nothing" (KJV), which appears to commend improvidence and indifference toward the future. A far more acceptable sense is provided in the 1904 edition, "Do not be anxious about anything." The RSV acknowledges the excellence of phrasing by revising only slightly, "Have no anxiety about anything," while the NRSV has, "Do not worry about anything."

From these few examples, it can be appreciated that the *Twentieth Century* translators rendered the English in a fresh way and created many phrases that have been adopted by later translators. Dr. Clark's final assessment is altogether valid. He wrote:

> When we read *The Twentieth Century New Testament* in its definitive form, it is difficult to remember that it was produced by so strange a company as we have met. Somewhere along the line, some transforming miracle seems to have occurred. We are forced to conclude that the devotion to their task has made them better scholars than they were at first. It is to their credit that they were always responsive to suggested revision, even to the last. Still it is amazing to find that the finest scholars of later years paid tribute to their work by adopting many of the same phrases and perceptive insights.[3]

Weymouth's *New Testament in Modern Speech* (1903)

Richard Francis Weymouth (1822–1902), a distinguished classical scholar, was a Baptist layman profoundly interested in the New Testament. In 1886 he published an edition of the Greek New Testament, presenting the text on which the majority of nineteenth-century editors were in agreement. He called this edition *The Resultant Greek Testament* (London: James Clarke & Co.). From 1869 to 1886, he was headmaster of Mill Hill School, London. Probably his work with the boys in the Mill Hill School

---

3. Clark, "The Making of the Twentieth Century New Testament," p. 81.

impressed upon his mind the need for a modern-speech version of the New Testament.

After his retirement in 1886, Weymouth proceeded to make such a translation based on his *Resultant Greek Testament*. His aim was to express the Greek text in the form the original writers would have used if writing in England at the close of the nineteenth century. The translation was completed in 1900, but ill health and finally his death in 1902 prevented his seeing it through the press. This task he entrusted to his friend Ernest Hampden-Cook, a Congregational minister, who had served as resident secretary of the Mill Hill School from 1891 to 1896. In 1903 James Clarke and Co. of London issued *The New Testament in Modern Speech*, with the subtitle *"An Idiomatic Translation into Everyday English from the Text of 'The Resultant Greek Testament'*; by the late Richard Francis Weymouth . . . edited and partly revised by Ernest Hampden-Cook." Besides revising the translation, Hampden-Cook also inserted headings and wrote some of the very numerous notes at the foot of every page. As previously mentioned, he had been one of the translators of *The Twentieth Century New Testament*.

Weymouth's rendering is couched in modern, dignified but often diffuse English and became especially popular in England. A fourth edition revised by three English scholars was published in 1924. One of the special features of Weymouth's linguistic work was the attention given to the exact rendering of the tenses of the Greek verb. His opinion "that—except in narrative—the aorist as a rule is *more* exactly rendered in English by our perfect with 'have' than by our simple past tense, and that in this particular the A.V. is in scores of instances more correct than the R.V." was convincingly set forth in a pamphlet entitled *On the Rendering into English of the Greek Aorist and Perfect* (London: James Clarke & Co., 1894).

The rendering of the Lord's Prayer (Matt. 6:9–13) will provide some idea of the nature of Weymouth's translation:

> Our Father in heaven, may Thy name be kept holy; let Thy kingdom come; let Thy will be done, as in Heaven so on earth; give us to-day bread for the day; and forgive us our shortcomings, as we also have forgiven those who have failed in their duty towards us; and bring us not into temptation, but rescue us from the Evil One.

Moffatt's Translation of the Bible (1913; 1924–25)

One of the most popular of the new versions has been that of James Moffatt (1870–1944), who translated the whole Bible into modern speech of free style. He prepared two different translations of the New Testament. The first preserved much of the language of the King James Version and was published at Edinburgh in 1901 in a volume entitled *The Historical New Testament*. This was a new translation of the documents of the New Testament arranged in their chronological order according to the critical literary theories of his time. The book won for him a doctor of divinity degree from the University of St. Andrews, which had never previously conferred the degree upon anyone so young.

Moffatt's second translation of the New Testament was issued in 1913 through Hodder & Stoughton, London, under the title *The New Testament: A New Translation*. As its title implies, it was an entirely fresh rendering and not a revision of the 1901 translation. Unfortunately, Moffatt's New Testament version was based on the Greek text that had been edited and published not long before by Hermann von Soden. This was a pity, for the more that von Soden's text was examined by textual critics, the more defects it was seen to contain.

In 1924–25 Moffatt surprised the English-speaking public with the publication of his new translation of the Old Testament, which was issued in two volumes. An edition of the complete Bible, incorporating the 1913 New Testament and the 1924–25 Old Testament, was published in London in one volume in 1926, and a revision was published in the United States in 1935.

In both Testaments, Moffatt felt at liberty to rearrange the sequence of verses and even chapters, supposedly restoring them to their "original position." The Gospel of John suffered more than any other book of the New Testament from this attempted restoration. John 3:22–30 is placed between 2:12 and 2:13. John 7:15–24 is moved to follow John 5:47. Within chapter 11 of John, verse 5 is placed between verses 2 and 3, and verses 18 and 19 are placed between verses 30 and 31. John 12:4–50 is put between 12:36a and 36b. Chapters 15 and 16 of John are "restored to their original position" between 13:31a and 31b. Finally, in chapter 18, verses 19 through 24 are placed between verses 14 and 15.

In the case of the Old Testament, Moffatt regarded the traditional text as "often desperately corrupt." Hence, nearly every page of his translation, he tells us, "contains some emendation of the traditional text."[4] At times he felt that the text was too defective to be restored, and he simply omitted such words and inserted ellipses (. . .).

Here and there in the New Testament, Moffatt adopted readings that have little manuscript support. But beyond that, he has accepted around thirty conjectural emendations without any manuscript support. There is no manuscript support for dropping from the text the words in 1 Timothy 5:23, "Give up being a total abstainer; take a little wine for the sake of your stomach and your frequent attacks of illness." Moffatt says in the footnote that the words are "either a marginal gloss or misplaced." In James 4:2 he accepts Erasmus's conjecture and reads "you covet," rather than "you kill." In 1 Peter 3:19 he introduces a new character into the puzzling passage about the spirits in prison by printing "Enoch also went and preached to the imprisoned spirits." Enoch is not mentioned in any of our authorities for the text, but William Bowyer (1772) anticipated a number of more recent scholars in suggesting that his name had fallen out by accident.

Nevertheless, as F. F. Bruce[5] concludes his evaluation of Moffatt's work, in spite of many criticisms that can quite justly be urged against the version, "it is but fair to say that to read through an Old Testament prophetical book or a New Testament epistle in his version is one of the best ways to get a grasp of the general argument."

Smith and Goodspeed's American Translation (1923; 1927)

Rivaling the Moffatt New Testament in value and popularity is the translation made by Edgar J. Goodspeed (1871–1962), professor of biblical and patristic Greek at the University of Chicago. His is a fairly free rendering and represents, as its subtitle indicates, *An American Translation*. As one of the most eloquent ad-

4. From Moffatt's introduction to his translation.
5. F. F. Bruce, *The English Bible: A History of Translations* (New York: Oxford University Press, 1970), p. 171.

vocates of modern-speech versions, Goodspeed declares in the preface to his rendering:

> The aim of the present translation has been to present the meaning of the different books as faithfully as possible, without bias or prejudice, in English of the same kind as the Greek of the original, so that they may be continuously and understandingly read. There is no book in the New Testament that cannot easily be read at a sitting. For American readers, especially, who have had to depend so long upon versions made in Great Britain, there is room for a New Testament free from expressions which, however familiar in England or Scotland, are strange to American ears.

Goodspeed based his translation on the Greek text of Westcott and Hort (1881). In eight places[6] he departed from this text. Three of these are conspicuous: the reading "on a pike" for "upon hyssop" in John 19:29; "Libyans" for "Libertines" (i.e., freedmen) in Acts 6:9; and the insertion of "Enoch" in 1 Peter 3:19. In the translation of the Letter to the Hebrews, there are a few curious slips in sentence arrangement: "the chest [ark] that contained the agreement [covenant], entirely covered with gold" (Heb. 9:4). It was the ark not the covenant that was gold-covered. Hebrews 10:1 reads: "the same sacrifices . . . cannot wholly free those who come to worship from their sins."

Within a matter of weeks, following the publication of Goodspeed's New Testament (1923), the University of Chicago Press approached him regarding a similar rendering of the Old Testament. Goodspeed referred the press to Professor J. M. Powis Smith of the Old Testament Department, who accepted the invitation to oversee such a translation.

For the task of the Old Testament translation, Smith sought the assistance of three other scholars who were graduates of the University of Chicago and were highly trained experts in Hebrew and related Semitic languages. They were Theophile J. Meek of the University of Toronto, Alexander R. Gordon of the United Theological College and McGill University, and Leroy Waterman of the University of Michigan. Smith served as editor.

6. The eight passages are John 19:29; Acts 6:9; 19:28, 34; James 1:17; 1 Pet. 3:19; Rev. 13:1; 15:6.

This translation was based on the traditional Hebrew text. The editor wrote, "Our guiding principle has been that the official Massoretic text must be adhered to as long as it made satisfactory sense. We have not tried to create a new text; but rather to translate the received text wherever translation was possible" (preface, p. xiii). An important feature of this edition of the Old Testament was the inclusion of an appendix of ninety-one closely printed pages indicating the passages where the translators departed from the Hebrew text as it now stands. In the introduction, they assured the reader that when they have rejected the received text, it is usually in order to adopt a better reading provided by the ancient versions and that they have adopted conjectural readings only "along generally approved lines." Published in 1927, this was the first version candidly to adopt conjectural emendations in its translation of the Hebrew text.

In 1931 Goodspeed's New Testament (1923) and Smith's Old Testament (1927), both published by the University of Chicago Press, were combined to form *The Bible: An American Translation*, with a short preface by Smith and Goodspeed. In 1933 an abridged edition, *The Short Bible*, was issued; the sections have brief introductions and are not in the normal biblical order. In 1938 Goodspeed also made a translation of the Apocrypha, and in 1939 this translation was included with the Old and New Testaments to form *The Complete Bible: An American Translation*.

In the preface to the Old Testament, the editor indicates that "the work of translation has been shared by four men. . . . Each of them carries the primary responsibility for his own work." He continues:

> The Editor has left his fellow-workers free to express themselves as they would, and has aimed at uniformity only in the most essential matters. If it be felt that each translator has his own style, this should not be regarded as a defect, for each document in the Old Testament has a style of its own, and the extent to which such stylistic characteristics are ignored by translators is a measure of their failure. Each book ought to speak its own message in its own way, even in a translation.

The four versions described in this chapter inaugurated the era of modern-speech Bibles in the twentieth century. Through them the English-reading public became accustomed to having the Scriptures in modern English. In addition, each of these versions has an intrinsic merit of its own and is still being used. They are all noteworthy also because of the contribution they made to the Revised Standard Version (1946–52). Two of the translators, Goodspeed and Moffatt, were members of the New Testament committee for the RSV, while Leroy Waterman was on the Old Testament committee. James Moffatt served as secretary for both committees until his death in 1944.

eight

—

The Revised Standard Version (1952)

The rapid multiplication of English translations of the Scriptures throughout the second half of the twentieth century might well prompt more than one bewildered reader to rephrase the Preacher's melancholy observation so as to read, "Of the making of many translations of the Bible there is no end!" (Eccles. 12:12). During the nearly forty years between the publication in 1952 of the Revised Standard Version and the publication in 1990 of the New Revised Standard Version, twenty-seven English renderings of the entire Bible were issued, as well as twenty-eight renderings of the New Testament alone.

Such a proliferation provokes a number of questions. Why have so many versions been produced? Was there really a need for such a variety of translations? Is it not uneconomical of time and human resources to undertake what, in many cases, are largely duplicated efforts? Irrespective of attempting to answer such questions, it will be useful to survey some of the reasons that led to the making of several of the English versions that are widely used today. These, in chronological order, are the Revised Standard Version (1952), the Jerusalem Bible (1966), the New American Bible (1970), the New English Bible (1970), the Good News Bible (1976), the New International Version (1978), the New King James Version (1982), the Contemporary English Version (1995), and the New International Reader's Version (1996). Several of these have subsequently appeared in revised form (see chap. 14).

Steps to produce a suitable revision of the excessively literalistic American Standard Version of 1901 were undertaken in 1928 when the copyright of that version was acquired by the International Council of Religious Education. In the same year, the Standard Bible Committee was appointed, with an original membership of fifteen scholars, to have charge of the text of the American Standard Version and to make further revision of the text should that be deemed necessary.

For two years the committee wrestled with the question of whether a revision should be undertaken, and if so, what should be its nature and extent. Finally, after revisions of representative chapters of the Bible had been made and discussed, a majority of the committee decided that there should be a thorough revision of the American Standard Version and that the revision should stay as close to the King James tradition as it could in the light of present knowledge of the Greek text and its meaning on the one hand, and present usage of English on the other.

In 1930 the United States was undergoing a serious economic depression, and it was not until 1936 that funds could be secured and the work of revision could begin in earnest. The contract was negotiated with Thomas Nelson and Sons, publishers of the American Standard Version, to finance the work of revision by advance royalties, in return for which the Nelsons were granted the exclusive right to publish the Revised Standard Version for a period of ten years. Thereafter, it was to be made available to other publishers under specific conditions.

With the financial undergirding thus provided, it was possible to schedule regular sessions of both the Old Testament and New Testament sections. Expenses for travel, lodging, and meals were provided for the members. No stipends or honoraria, however, were given to committee members, who contributed their time and expertise for the good of the cause.

After serious work had begun, a hope was expressed that the cooperation of British scholars might be obtained, thus making the version an international translation. The war years of 1939–45, however, made such collaboration impossible. In the summer of 1946, an effort was made to secure at least a token of international collaboration in the work on the Old Testament, the RSV New Testament having been published in February 1946. Such partial collaboration, however, was not to be forthcoming, for in that same year delegates of several Protestant churches in Great Britain decided that work should begin on a wholly new translation, one that made no attempt to stand within the tradition of the 1611 King James Bible. The outcome of this effort was the New English Bible, published in 1970 (see pp. 132–37 below).

Meanwhile, work continued on the RSV Old Testament. After eighty-one separate meetings totaling 450 days of work, the complete Bible was published September 30, 1952, the feast day, appropriately enough, of St. Jerome. The new version was launched with an unprecedented publicity campaign. On the evening of the day of publication, in the United States, Canada, and many other places, 3,418 community observances were held with over one and a half million persons attending.

The fanfare, however, did not protect the new version from adverse criticism. Unfounded and malicious accusations were brought against several members of the committee, alleging that they were either Communists or Communist sympathizers—allegations that, at the insistence of Senator Joseph McCarthy of Wisconsin, were eventually printed in the official United States Air Force Training Manual! Finally, after a thorough investigation conducted by nonpartisan authorities, this entirely unsupported charge was rebutted as "venomous nonsense" on the floor of the House of Representatives in Washington, and the edition of the manual in question was withdrawn.[1]

Charges of modernism were leveled against the revisers because, for example, the phrase "through his blood" was no longer included in Colossians 1:14. In this case, it was overlooked that the

1. *The Congressional Record*, vol. 106, part 3 (February 25, 1960), 3505–7; part 5 (March 29, 1960), 6872–74; and part 6 (April 19, 1960), 8247–84.

words are not present in the oldest and best manuscripts, that they got into the Textus Receptus by scribal conflation with the parallel passage in Ephesians 1:7, and that in 1901 the American Standard Version had already eliminated the spurious words.

Meanwhile, a pastor of a church in Rocky Mount, North Carolina, publicly burned with a blowtorch a copy of what he termed "a heretical, communist-inspired Bible." The ashes were put in a metal box and sent to Luther Weigle, dean of Yale University Divinity School, who had served as convener of the Standard Bible Committee. That box, with its contents, is with the Bible Committee's collection of books and archives, a reminder that, though in previous centuries Bible translators were sometimes burned, today it is happily only a copy of the translation that meets such a fate.[2]

In 1971 the second edition of the RSV New Testament was issued. This incorporated a number of changes reflecting the Greek text that had been adopted for the forthcoming third edition of the United Bible Societies' *Greek New Testament* (1975), which serves throughout the world as a standard text for translation and revisions made by Protestants and Roman Catholics alike. Among such changes was the transfer of the ending of the Gospel according to Mark and the *pericope de adultera* (John 7:53–8:11) from the RSV footnotes into the text, though the passages continue to be separated from the context by a blank space with explanatory notes to indicate that they were not part of the original text.

Soon afterward, a significant step was taken by scholars of the Catholic Biblical Association of Great Britain. Under the leadership of Dom Bernard Orchard, O.S.B., and Father Reginald C. Fuller, a proposal was made to divide the books of the Apocrypha into two sections, one containing those books the Catholic Church regards as deuterocanonical and one containing those that are not so regarded. In an edition issued by Collins Press of Glasgow in 1973, these two sections were bound separately between the Old and New Testaments. The volume therefore had four sections: the thirty-nine books of the Old Testament, the twelve deuterocanonical books or parts of books, the First and Second Books of Esdras

---

2. See Paul J. Thuesen, *In Discordance with the Scriptures: American Protestant Battles over Translating the Bible* (New York: Oxford University Press, 1999), pp. 93–119.

and the Prayer of Manasseh (three books that are part of the traditional Apocrypha but are not included among the deuterocanonical books), and the twenty-seven books of the New Testament. No Catholic notes were included, since the Bible was to be "common," for use by Roman Catholics and Protestants alike.

It should be noted that in agreeing to such an arrangement, Roman Catholics made a significant departure from the accepted practice through the long history of their church. The separation of the deuterocanonical books from their places throughout the Old Testament is essentially an accommodation to the Protestant arrangement of the books of the Bible.

In May 1973 a specially bound copy of the Collins RSV "Common" Bible was presented to Pope Paul VI. In a private audience granted to a small group, comprising the Greek Orthodox Archbishop Athenagoras of London, Lady Priscilla Collins, Sir William Collins, Herbert G. May, and the present writer, the pope accepted the copy as a significant step in furthering ecumenical relations among the churches.

Worthy as the "Common" Bible is, however, it fails to live up to its name, for it lacks the full canon of books recognized as authoritative by Eastern Orthodox churches. The Greek, Russian, Ukrainian, Bulgarian, Serbian, Armenian, and other Eastern churches accept not only the traditional deuterocanonical books received by the Roman Catholic Church but also the Third Book of Maccabees. Furthermore, in Greek Bibles Psalm 151 stands at the close of the Psalter, and the Fourth Book of Maccabees is printed as an appendix to the Old Testament. Since these texts were lacking in the "Common" Bible presented to Pope Paul, on that occasion Archbishop Athenagoras expressed to the present writer the hope that steps might be taken to produce a truly ecumenical edition of the Holy Scriptures.

In 1972 a subcommittee of the RSV Bible Committee had already been commissioned to prepare a translation of 3 and 4 Maccabees and Psalm 151. In 1975 the translation of the three additional texts was made available to the five publishers licensed to issue the RSV Bible. The Oxford University Press in New York immediately took steps to produce an expanded form of *The New Oxford Annotated Bible, with the Apocrypha,* the edition of the RSV that had earlier received the imprimatur of Cardinal Cushing of Boston.

This expanded edition was published by the Oxford University Press on May 19, 1977. A special prepublication copy was presented by the present writer to His All Holiness Dimitrios I, the ecumenical patriarch of Constantinople and titular head of the several Orthodox Churches. In accepting the gift, the ecumenical patriarch expressed satisfaction at the availability of an edition of the sacred Scriptures that English readers belonging to all branches of the Christian church could use.

Thus, the story of the making of the Revised Standard Version of the Bible with the expanded Apocrypha is an account of the triumph of ecumenical concern over more limited sectarian interests. Now, for the first time since the Reformation, one edition of the Bible had received the blessing of leaders of Protestant, Roman Catholic, and Eastern Orthodox churches alike.

For a discussion of the New Revised Standard Version, see pages 155–62 below.

—

nine

The Jerusalem Bible (1966)

The name, The Jerusalem Bible, indicates something of the origin of this version. Beginning in 1948, a group of French Dominicans and others at the École biblique de Jérusalem produced a series of biblical commentaries issued in forty-three fascicles, each containing one or more books of the Bible translated into the vernacular, with introductions of moderate length and copious notes. In 1956, two years after the completion of the series, a one-volume edition was issued, in which the notes were greatly compressed and the introduction sharply abbreviated. This compendious edition, entitled *La Sainte Bible traduite en français sous la direction de l'École biblique de Jérusalem,* contains, therefore, the quintessence of a great amount of solid and responsible scholarship contributed by about forty collaborators.

An English edition was prepared by twenty members of the British Catholic Biblical Association under the direction of Alex-

ander Jones of Christ's College, Liverpool; it embodies the introductions and notes of the one-volume French edition. The
translation of the scriptural text of most of the books was made
from the original languages, and, in the case of a few books
where the initial draft had been made from the French, it was
later "compared word for word with the Hebrew or Aramaic by
the General Editor and amended where necessary to ensure
complete conformity with the ancient text" (p. v). It was perhaps inevitable that the names of the original scholars who produced the *Bible de Jérusalem* have been replaced by the names of
the nearly thirty British collaborators in the work of translation
and literary revision.

This historic work breaks from Jerome's Vulgate and is the first
complete Roman Catholic Bible in English translated from the original languages. It is also the first to take major advantage of the
Dead Sea Scrolls thus far discovered. Its objective, as stated in the
editor's foreword, is "to serve two pressing needs facing the Church,
the need to keep abreast of the times and the need to deepen theological thought." The English translators attempted to meet the first
by "translating the ancient text into the language we use today,"
and the second by providing notes that are "neither sectarian nor
superficial."

So much by the way of describing the background and production of the Jerusalem Bible; something should be said now about
the scholarship reflected in both translation and comments. Let it
be said at the outset that during the past generation the differences
between the results of Protestant and Roman Catholic biblical
scholarship had been reduced almost to the vanishing point, and a
great expanse of common ground now existed in questions pertaining to date, authorship, literary composition, and similar matters of biblical studies.

The wording of the Jerusalem Bible (1966) has a contemporary
ring about it. The archaic forms of the second person pronouns
("thee," "thy," "thine," "ye") are dispensed with. The Song of
Songs is presented as a drama composed of five poems with speaking parts for bride, bridegroom, and chorus. Goliath was one of the
Philistine "shock-troopers" (1 Sam. 17:4). The editor acknowledges that the decision, reached after some hesitation, to represent
the divine name by "Yahweh" may seem to many readers to be

unacceptable, but "those who may care to use this translation of the Psalms can substitute the traditional 'the Lord'" (p. vi).

The passage in Isaiah 7:14 is rendered, "The maiden is with child and will soon give birth to a son," to which the following comment is attached: "The Greek version reads 'the virgin,' being more explicit than the Heb. which uses *almah*, meaning either a young girl or a young recently married, woman." In the annunciation (Luke 1:28), the words of the angel Gabriel to Mary are rendered, "Rejoice, so highly favoured! The Lord is with you," with the added comment, "The translation 'Rejoice' may be preferred to 'Hail' and regarded as containing a messianic reference, cf. Zc 9:9; 'so highly favoured,' i.e. as to become the mother of the Messiah." The New Testament references to the *adelphoi* of Jesus are rendered in a straightforward manner, "the brothers of Jesus," with the added comment at Matthew 12:46, "Not Mary's children but near relations, cousins perhaps, which both Hebr. and Aramaic style 'brothers,' cf. Gn 13:8; 14:16; 29:15; Lv 10:4; 1 Ch 23:22 f."

Occasionally, the translators have ventured to paraphrase, sometimes not altogether happily. Thus, 1 Corinthians 7:1–2 is rendered, "Now for the questions about which you wrote. Yes, it is a good thing for a man not to touch a woman; but since sex is always a danger, let each man have his own wife and each woman her own husband." Here the opening of verse 2 is given an unfortunate twist ("but since sex is always a danger"); literally, the Greek reads "but because of fornications," which probably means "but because there is so much sexual immorality." This was certainly true in Corinth.

Since in various passages the manuscripts of the Bible differ from one another, translators must make choices among variant readings. In the textual criticism of the New Testament, the Jerusalem Bible usually reflects current judgments widely held among Protestant and most Roman Catholic scholars. Thus, the ending of Mark's Gospel (16:9–20), which is lacking in the earliest witnesses, is declared to be probably non-Marcan, and the *pericope de adultera* (John 7:53–8:11) is recognized as not being part of the original fourth Gospel, for "it is omitted by the oldest witnesses (MSS, versions, Fathers) and found elsewhere in others; moreover, its style is that of the Synoptics and the author was possibly Luke. Nevertheless, the passage was accepted in the canon and there are no grounds for regarding it as unhistorical." The comment on John 5:3b–4 states that "the best witnesses omit 'waiting for the water to move' and the whole of v. 4."

In these three cases, the passage is retained in the text; in 1 John 5:7b–8, however, the spurious passage is given only in the comments, where it is recognized that the reference to the Trinity is probably a gloss that crept into inferior manuscripts of the Latin Vulgate. In these cases, the Jerusalem Bible agrees with the mainstream of textual scholarship. On the other hand, the text-critical judgment expressed at John 1:13, though previously advocated by a few scholars, is scarcely correct. Here the translators abandoned the evidence of all Greek manuscripts and, on the basis of several Old Latin and Syriac manuscripts, with limited patristic support, they adopted the singular number, "who was born," thus making the Fourth Gospel testify to the virgin birth of Christ.

In 1975 an edition of the Jerusalem Bible Version entitled *The Bible in Order* was published in New York by Doubleday. The editor, Joseph Rhymer of Notre Dame College, Bearsden, Glasgow, provided an extensive subtitle: *All the writings which make up the Bible, arranged in their chronological order according to the dates at which they were written, or edited into the form in which we know them; seen against the history of the times, as the Bible provides it. With Introductions and Notes.*

For a discussion of The New Jerusalem Bible (1985), see page 151 below.

ten

—

The New American Bible (1970)

In 1944 the Bishops' Committee of the Confraternity of Christian Doctrine invited a group of Catholic biblical scholars to undertake the first Roman Catholic translation of the Scriptures in America to be made from the original languages. The committee inherited the work that had been started in the preceding decade, when many of the same group of scholars began translating the Bible from the Latin Vulgate (the New Testament of their version had been published in 1941).

During the following years, several portions of the new translation appeared, each containing one or more biblical books. The reissuing of these earlier materials permitted the introduction of certain modifications. For example, the Book of Genesis, first published in 1952, was completely retranslated and provided with new and expanded exegetical notes that took into account the various sources or literary traditions. Finally, in 1970, a quarter of a century after work first began, The New American Bible was published. This version represents capable and dedicated scholarship and provides a rendering of the Scriptures in modern American idiom, along with a brief introduction to each biblical book as well as many literary and theological annotations.

In the Old Testament, the translators departed more than a few times from the Masoretic Hebrew text. According to information in the preface, the Masoretic Hebrew text of 1 and 2 Samuel was in numerous instances corrected by the more ancient Hebrew manuscripts from Cave 4 of Qumran. In the case of the Psalms, the basic text was not the Masoretic text but "one which the editors considered closer to the original inspired form, namely, the Hebrew text underlying the new Latin Psalter of the Church" (the reference is to the *Liber Psalmorum cum Canticis Breviarii Romani,* 2d ed., 1945).

Here and there in the Old Testament and particularly in the Minor Prophets, the sequence of verses has been changed, and sections of material have been rearranged where scholars have reason to think that lines were accidentally disordered in the transmission of the text. With regard to the Tetragrammaton, happily the translators have used "LORD" rather than the utterly un-English "Yahweh."

With regard to fitness of language, the Book of Psalms gives the impression that meticulous care was taken to provide a rendering with a certain liturgical and literary timbre. In general the language is dignified without being archaic, and expressions are used that evoke a sense of grandeur and the numinous. Only rarely have the translators nodded, as when, for example, in Psalm 24:1 what is meaningful to the eye will almost certainly be confusing to the ear: "The LORD's are the earth and its fullness."

In other parts of the Bible, the reader is struck by a certain typically American quality of English idiom—plain, flat, and matter-of-fact. The long and involved Greek sentences in Ephesians (e.g., one sentence extends from 1:3 to 1:14) and in other epistles are properly broken into smaller units. At the same time, one can point out a number of rather uninspired, pedestrian renderings. For example, it is difficult to regard the following as idiomatic or felicitous English: "Be on the lookout against the yeast of the Pharisees and Sadducees" (Matt. 16:6); "for fear of disedifying them [the kings of the world]" (17:27); "Buy ointment to smear on your eyes" (Rev. 3:18).

As is true of most translations of the Bible prepared by a committee, the several books of the New American Bible are the work of different translators. In such cooperative work, therefore, it is not surprising to find differences among the books as to the technique of translating and the style or "color" of the rendering. To some extent, the reader of the New American Bible is forewarned of such diversity by the statement in the preface that "the editors did not commit themselves in the synoptic gospels to rendering repeated words or phrases identically."

On the other hand, it is hard to justify the many apparently arbitrary divergences in the rendering of technical or quasi-technical words and phrases. For example, the Greek word *makarios* is translated "blest" in the Matthean and Lukan beatitudes, whereas in the seven beatitudes contained in the Book of Revelation it is rendered "happy." The expression *hē basileia tou theou* occurs forty-six times in Mark and Luke. Sixteen times it is rendered "the kingdom of God," once "God's kingdom," once "kingdom of heaven" (!), and the remaining instances "the reign of God." Within a single chapter (Luke 18) and even in adjacent verses, one finds the following disparate renderings (italicized here): "Let the little children come to me. Do not shut them off. *The reign of God* belongs to such as these" (v. 16). "Trust me when I tell you that whoever does not accept *the kingdom of God* as a child will not enter into it" (v. 17). "It is easier for a camel to go through a needle's eye than for a rich man to enter *the kingdom of heaven*" (v. 25). "There is no one who has left home or wife or brothers, parents or children, for the sake of *the kingdom of God* . . ." (v. 29). A similar type of arbitrary divergence occurs in Matthew 3:2 and 4:17. In the former passage, John the Baptizer preaches, "Reform your lives! The reign of God is at hand," and in the latter Jesus begins to preach, "Reform your lives! The kingdom of heaven is at hand." In both cases, the Greek has *hē basileia tōn ouranōn*.

[handwritten margin note: Different Translation]

It is difficult to believe that the committee of translators (who were technically trained scholars) would have been guilty of perpetrating such slipshod work. One may hazard the guess that, after the scholars had finished their painstaking work, having utilized a concordance and a harmony of the Gospels to make certain that parallels are treated as parallels, the subcommittee on English style made quite arbitrary alterations here and there, which, perhaps because of the press of time in meeting the publisher's deadline, were not submitted to the scholars for their final approval.

As would be expected, an edition of the Scriptures prepared by Roman Catholic scholars will contain various kinds of explanatory notes. It is interesting to examine those that bear on what has come to be termed the *sensus plenior* ("fuller sense") of Scripture. This is understood as the deeper meaning intended by God (but not clearly intended by the human author) seen to exist in the words of Scripture when they are studied in the light of further revelation or of development in the understanding of revelation.

The messianic interpretation of various Old Testament passages is suggested both by annotations and by section headings. The lengthy annotation on Genesis 3:15 concludes with the statement that "the passage can be understood as the first promise of a Redeemer for fallen mankind. The woman's offspring then is primarily Jesus Christ." At Genesis 49:10, which by a slight change in the Hebrew text is translated, "While tribute is brought to him [Judah]," one is told that "a somewhat different reading of the Hebrew text would be 'until he comes to whom it belongs.' This last has been traditionally understood in a Messianic sense. In any case, the passage foretells the supremacy of the tribe of Judah, which found its fulfillment in the Davidic dynasty and ultimately in the Messianic Son of David, Jesus Christ." Of Balaam's prophecy that "a star shall advance from Jacob" (Num. 24:17), the reader learns that "many of the Fathers have understood this as a Messianic prophecy, although it is not referred to anywhere in the New Testament; in this sense the star is Christ himself, just as he is the staff from Israel; cf Is 11,1." Psalm 45 is described as a "Nuptual Ode for the Messianic King," and the annotation declares that "Catholic tradition, in keeping with the inspired interpretation given in Heb 1,8f, has always understood this psalm as referring, at least in a typical sense, to Christ and his bride, the church." Psalm 72 is given the heading "The Kingdom of the Messiah." Both Isaiah 52:13–53:12 and Psalm 22 are applied to the Passion of Christ. The words "the Lord begot me, the firstborn of his ways" (Prov. 8:22), so hotly debated during the Arian controversies in the early church, is furnished with an annotation that concludes with the statement, "Here that plurality of divine Persons is foreshadowed which was afterward to be fully revealed when Wisdom in the Person of Jesus Christ became incarnate."

The controversial passage of Isaiah 7:14, which is translated, "The virgin shall be with child, and bear a son, and shall name him Immanuel," has, as one would expect, a lengthy annotation, part of which is quoted here:

> The church has always followed St. Matthew in seeing the transcendent fulfillment of this verse in Christ and his Virgin Mother. The prophet need not have known the full force latent in his own words; and some Catholic writers have sought a preliminary and partial fulfillment in the conception and birth of the future King Hezekiah, whose mother, at the time Isaiah spoke, would have been a young, unmarried woman (Hebrew, almah). The Holy Spirit was preparing, however, for another Nativity which alone could fulfill the divinely given terms of Immanuel's mission, and in which the perpetual virginity of the Mother of God was to fulfill also the words of this prophecy in the integral sense intended by the divine Wisdom.

For a discussion of the revised edition of the New Testament of The New American Bible, see pages 152–53 below.

—

eleven

The New English Bible (1970)

In May 1946 the General Assembly of the Church of Scotland received an overture from the Presbytery of Stirling and Dunblane recommending that a translation of the Bible be made in the language of the present day. After several months of negotiating with representatives of other major Protestant denominations of Great Britain, as well as the university presses of Oxford and Cambridge, a joint committee was formed that entrusted the actual work of translation to four panels of scholars, dealing respectively with the Old Testament, the Apocrypha, the New Testament, and the literary revision of the whole. The convener of the panel of Old Testament scholars was G. R. Driver of Oxford University; the convener of the Apocrypha panel was G. D. Kilpatrick, also of Oxford; and C. H. Dodd, professor emeritus of Cambridge University, served as convener of the New Testament panel and as general director of the entire project.[1]

1. For further details, see Geoffrey Hunt, ed., *About the New English Bible* (London: Oxford University Press and Cambridge University Press, 1970).

The procedure adopted for the work of the panels was as follows. Each book or group of books was assigned to an individual translator, who did not need to be a member of one of the four panels. The first draft of the translation was circulated in typescript to members of the appropriate panels, who worked through it individually and jointly in committee sessions along with the translator. When the draft had been thoroughly discussed and revised, perhaps several times, it went to the literary panel for suggestions on improving the English style. The final form of the version was reached by agreement between the two panels.

The New English Bible is a totally fresh translation; it is not a revision of earlier versions. The aim of the translators was to cut loose from all previous renderings and to "render the Greek, as we understood it, into the English of the present day, that is, into the natural vocabulary, constructions, and rhythms of contemporary speech. We have sought to avoid archaism, jargon, and all that is either stilted or slipshod."[2] The result is a version marked by a vigorous and colorful English style, tending at places to be periphrastic with interpretive additions.

Work on the New Testament was finished first, and the volume was published in 1961. What struck most reviewers was the freedom of rendering and the insertion of words for which there is no express warrant in the text (for convenience of explanation, the inserted words are italicized here; they are not italicized in the NEB): "Those who sleep *in death*" (1 Thess. 4:13); "in *the province of* Asia" (Rev. 1:4); "in his body of flesh *and blood* (Col. 1:22); "*guardian* angel" (Matt. 18:10; Acts 12:15); "*human* body" (Rom. 12:4); "his *life's* blood" (Rev. 1:5); "tongues *of ecstasy*" (1 Cor. 13:8). In other cases, the literal rendering is supplanted altogether by a periphrasis. Thus "scribes" becomes "doctors of the law" (Mark 15:31, etc.), the parable of the talents is now the parable of "the bags of gold" (Matt. 25:14–30), the word traditionally translated "saints" is rendered "God's people" (Col. 1:2, etc.), "beloved" as a term of address becomes "dear friends" (1 John 4:7, etc.), and the verb "it is written" (Rom. 12:19) becomes "there is a text which reads." In view of such freedom in rendering the text, the principal reviewer of the New Testament of the New English Bible in *The*

2. Introduction to the NEB New Testament (1961), p. x.

Times Literary Supplement (London) concluded his review with the words, "If one's sole concern is what the New Testament writers mean, it [the new version] is excellent. It is otherwise if one wants to find out what the documents actually say."[3]

Among details concerning readings and renderings in the Old Testament, which was published in 1970, the following are of special interest. The text of certain Old Testament passages has been rearranged in accordance with what some scholars regard as a more suitable sequence, notably in Isaiah and Zechariah. Occasionally, square brackets are employed (e.g., Job 11:6b) to designate material considered to be late additions to the original text.

In the Song of Songs (this Hebraism has been retained), the identity of the speakers has been indicated by placing in the left margin the words "Bridegroom," "Bride," and "Companions." These helpful notations, printed in italics, have been derived (and slightly corrected) from two manuscripts of the Septuagint. On the other hand, one can only express regret that the panel of translators decided to omit the Masoretic headings of the Psalms. It is true that many of the musical notations in the headings are among the most difficult linguistic problems that confront the Hebrew lexicographer, but this is no reason why at least an attempt at rendering them should not have been made.

In Ezekiel the traditional expression "son of man," used frequently in addressing the prophet, has been rendered idiomatically by "man." Typical examples are the following: "And now, man, a word for you" (24:25); "Man, look towards the Ammonites" (25:1); "Man, prophesy and say . . ." (30:1); "Man, can these bones live again?" (37:3), etc. Such expressions remind American readers of hippie and African-American usage popular in the 1960s.

The Hebrew *ḥesed* is translated in a variety of ways: "strong love" (Ps. 103:11), "true love" (Ps. 138:8), "faithful friendship" (1 Sam. 20:14), "loyalty" (Mic. 6:8), and so on. In Isaiah 7:14 *ʾalmah*, as would be expected, is rendered "a young woman," and in Isaiah 52:14 the words "my people," which are not in the Hebrew, have been added in accordance with the translators' interpretation of the passage.

3. 24 March 1961, p. 178.

The books of the Apocrypha were assigned to a committee originally under the chairmanship of Professor G. D. Kilpatrick and
latterly under the chairmanship of W. D. McHardy, Regius Professor of Hebrew at Oxford (who also served since 1968 as deputy director of the entire project). The translation of 1 and 2 Maccabees
has been provided (as is the case also in the RSV) with footnotes
giving dates in terms of years B.C. The title of the treatise traditionally known as Bel and the Dragon now appears as Daniel, Bel, and
the Snake. In 2 Esdras the variant readings of the Oriental versions (Syriac, Armenian, Georgian, Ethiopic, and two forms of Arabic) are not precisely identified (as they are in the RSV) but are
listed anonymously as "Vss."

During the decade since the New Testament was published, a
great many criticisms and suggestions had been offered by various
reviewers.[4] The New Testament panel, still under the chairmanship of C. H. Dodd, having given serious attention to such criticisms, introduced almost four hundred alterations and corrections
into the second edition of the New Testament, which was published in 1970 along with the Old Testament. Some of these are of
a purely stylistic nature, such as those in the nativity account in
Luke 2:1–14. In verse 1, "a general registration" has become in the
second edition "a registration"; verse 5, "to be registered" becomes
"to register"; verse 6, "[Mary] was pregnant" becomes "[Mary]
was expecting a child" (Rev. 12:2 still reads, "She was pregnant")
and "her child" becomes "her baby"; verse 7, "She wrapped him
round" becomes "She wrapped him in his swaddling clothes"; and
in verse 12, "all wrapped up" becomes "wrapped in his swaddling
clothes."

Other helpful changes were introduced into the second edition
of the New Testament. "Do not feed your pearls to pigs" (Matt.
7:6) has become, more appropriately, "Do not throw your pearls
to the pigs." The promise of Jesus that "the forces of death shall
never overpower" the church (Matt. 16:18) is now "the powers of
death shall never conquer it." In Matthew 20:31, "the people
rounded on them [the blind men]" has been altered to "the people
told them sharply to be quiet." In a similar way, Timothy is now
advised to "charge them solemnly before God" (2 Tim. 2:14), in-

4. See, e.g., the volume edited by D. E. Nineham, *The New English Bible
Reviewed* (London: Epworth, 1965).

stead of to "adjure them before God," and in the following sentence, "be straightforward in your proclamation of the truth" replaces "driving a straight furrow in your proclamation of the truth."

Finally, it is not without interest that several significant alterations were introduced into the introduction to the New Testament, which is signed with the initials of C. H. Dodd. For example, no longer is the reader informed (as was true in the 1961 edition) that "in no passage of doubtful meaning does the rendering adopted represent merely the preference of any single person." Again, in the discussion of the fine line between translation and paraphrase, the older statement read: "But if paraphrase means taking the liberty of introducing into a passage something which is not there, to elucidate the meaning which is there, it can be said that we have taken this liberty only with extreme caution, and in a very few passages. . . ." This has become in the second edition: "We have had recourse to deliberate paraphrase with great caution, and only in a few passages. . . ."

These examples will illustrate the kinds of alterations introduced into the second edition of the New Testament. Perhaps some will think that the revision was too cautious, and that occasional Britishisms or recherché expressions might well have been removed. Thus, the reader of the NEB still learns that Stephen's speech "touched them [those who heard] on the raw" (Acts 7:54), and Paul still advises the Corinthians to "have nothing to do with loose livers" (1 Cor. 5:9). In Mark 4:21 the lamp is still put "under the meal-tub," and in 6:3 we are still told that the congregation that heard Jesus teach in the synagogue "fell foul of him." A particularly notable example of the use of unusual and non-colloquial English is the rendering of Revelation 18:16, where the merchants and traders lament the fall of Babylon in stilted language: "Alas, alas for the great city . . . bedizened with gold and jewels and pearls!"—whereas the so-called archaic King James Version uses the perfectly good word "decked."

With regard to the overall style of the New English Bible, one finds a mixture. To give their rendering contemporary flavor, the translators include an occasional colloquialism, such as, "they hasten hot-foot into crime" (Prov. 1:16), and, "This is more than we can stomach" (John 6:60). On the other hand, one notices also a tendency to use pedantically precise words, as well as rare and unusual ones. Examples include asphodel, batten, distrain, felloe, hoopoes, keen (as a verb), lapis lazuli, panniers, reck, ruffed bustard, runnels of water, and stook.

For a discussion of a revision of the New English Bible, see pages 153–55 below.

twelve

—

The New International
Version (1978)

As was mentioned earlier, when the Revised Standard Version appeared in 1952, it received severe criticism from some who regarded themselves as conservative in theology and politics. Subsequently, several Bibles were published under conservative auspices (e.g., the Amplified Bible in 1965, the Modern Language Bible in 1969, and the New American Standard Bible in 1971), but none of them succeeded in becoming the standard Bible for conservative Protestants.

The effort that finally culminated in such a version began in the 1950s, when committees were appointed by the Synod of the Christian Reformed Church (in 1956) and the National Association of Evangelicals (in 1957) to study the feasibility of preparing a new translation. In 1961 the two committees met together and merged as a joint committee. Over the next few years, additional scholars became interested and were added to the committee, and in 1968 Edwin H. Palmer became the full-time executive secretary of the project. Work began in 1968, and the Gospel of John was published in 1969; in 1973 the New Testament was issued. Finally, after several Old Testament books appeared separately, the entire Bible was finished in 1978.[1]

The publicity released with the publication of this translation stressed the interdenominational and international character of the work. The preface (p. vii) lists thirteen different denominations represented. As for the countries represented, a pamphlet *The Version of Our Time* gives a "partial list" of ninety-seven persons, of whom eighty-seven were Americans; there were three each from Canada and Great Britain, and two each from Australia and New Zealand. These worked in twenty teams, each of which was composed of five persons: two co-translators, two consultants, and one English stylist. Each team's work went to an intermediate editorial committee (either of the Old Testament or the New Testament), then to the general editorial committee, and finally to the fifteen-member committee on Bible translation.

Early in the development of plans for the project, financial backing for the work was promised by the New York Bible Society. It is understandable that the hourly wages for more than a hundred translators, the cost of their transportation as well as accommodation of room and board for the many months they met in committee, the many incidental expenses for secretarial labor, duplicating equipment, and other items eventually surpassed the budget that the New York Bible Society was able to provide. Another source of revenue became available when the Zondervan Bible Publishers, having contracted with the New York Bible Society to be the sole commercial publisher in America for the new translation, advanced funds to help defray the costs. Eventually, according to James Powell, then president of the newly renamed International Bible Society, the total editorial cost would reach approximately eight million dollars.[2]

1. See Kenneth L. Barker, ed., *The NIV: The Making of a Contemporary Translation* (Grand Rapids: Zondervan, 1986); also issued as *The Making of a Contemporary Translation: New International Version* (London: Hodder & Stoughton, 1987).

2. Burton L. Goddard, *The NIV Story: The Inside Story of the New International Version* (New York: Vantage, 1989), p. 100.

From the beginning, emphasis was placed on the translators' high view of Scripture. The New Testament preface states that they were all committed to "the full authority and complete trustworthiness of the Scriptures, which they believe to be God's Word in written form." The preface to the Bible declares that "the translators were united in their commitment to the authority and infallibility of the Bible as God's Word in written form."

The external features of the printed volume are pleasing. The text is printed in one column; the use of poetic structure is frequent and effective. The text is divided into sections, with section headings.

A rather unusual device is the use of quotation marks to set off a word or phrase that the translators judged was being used in a sense different from the normal one. Examples include "sinners" in Matthew 9:10–11 (and parallels); "gods" in Psalm 82:1, 6, as well as the quotation in John 10:34; "acts of righteousness" in Matthew 9:10–11; and (rather curiously) the bracketing of "seven(s)" within quotation marks in Daniel 9:24–27.

For some reason, "Mary Magdalene" is used in the Synoptic Gospels, but in John she appears as "Mary of Magdala." Another inconsistency involves the manner in which units of time are indicated. In the Gospels the form of the Greek is maintained ("the third hour," "the sixth hour," etc.), but in Acts there is a shift to the modern way of telling time: "nine in the morning" (2:15); "three in the afternoon" (3:1; 10:3, 30); "about noon" (19:9); and "at nine tonight" (23:23).

It is surprising that translators who profess to have "a high view of Scripture" should take liberties with the text by omitting words or, more often, by adding words that are not in the manuscripts. At the beginning of the Sermon on the Mount (Matt. 5:2), the NIV omits the words included in all Greek manuscripts that Jesus "opened his mouth and"—without providing any English equivalent for the phrase. On the other hand, in Jeremiah 7:22 the translators have inserted the word "just" for which there is no Hebrew authority. In the New Testament at Matthew 13:32 concerning the mustard seed, they inserted the word "your" ("the smallest of all your seeds") and the word "now" in 1 Peter 4:6 ("the gospel was preached even to those who are now dead")—neither of which is in the Greek text. In 1 Corinthians 4:9, we find in the NIV a quite considerable elaboration of what Paul actually wrote: "God

put us apostles on display *at the end of the procession,* like men condemned to die *in the arena*" (the two additions have been italicized
here).[3]

The New International Version is more colloquial than the Revised Standard Version, less free than the New English Bible, and
more literary than the Good News Bible.

For the New International Reader's Version (NIrv), see pages 171–
74 below.

---

3. For many more examples of such changes in the NIV, see Robert P. Martin,
Accuracy of Translation and the New International Version (Carlisle, Pa.: Banner of
Truth Trust, 1989), pp. 19–67; and Earl D. Radmacher and Zane C. Hodges, *The
NIV Reconsidered: A Fresh Look at a Popular Translation* (Dallas: Rendención Viva,
1990), pp. 25–130.

thirteen

—

Jewish Translations

Translations Sponsored by the Jewish Publication Society (1917; 1985)

In 1917 the Jewish Publication Society of America in Philadelphia issued *The Holy Scriptures according to the Masoretic Text*, a rendering of the Hebrew Bible bearing a close affinity to the idiom of the King James Version and the Revised Version of the nineteenth century. According to the preface (p. vii),

The present translation is the first for which a group of men representative of Jewish learning among English-speaking Jews assume joint responsibility, all previous efforts in the English language having been the work of individual translators. It has a character of its own. It aims to combine the spirit of Jewish tradition with the results of biblical scholarship, ancient, mediaeval, and modern. It gives to the Jewish world a translation of the Scriptures done by men imbued with the Jewish consciousness, while the non-Jewish world, it is hoped, will welcome a translation that presents many passages from the Jewish traditional point of view.

Although the 1917 version satisfied the needs of the English-speaking Jewish community for several decades, by the middle of the twentieth century it became apparent that a new version was needed, one that would speak in a twentieth-century idiom to modern readers and would embody the latest discoveries in understanding the Scriptures. In 1955 a committee of seven Jewish scholars began work to produce such a version.

By September 1962, *The Torah,* the first section of the Hebrew Scriptures, was issued in a totally new translation. The second part of the Hebrew canon, *The Prophets,* was issued in 1978 in a single volume, and *The Writings* in 1982. Finally, a one-volume edition of the three parts was published in 1985. This was called *Tanakh,* the traditional acronym for the three parts of the Hebrew Bible, *Torah* (Law), *Nebiʾim* (Prophets), and *Kethubim* (Writings), thus *TNK,* or *Tanakh*—the Holy Scriptures. The personnel of the committee that translated the Writings comprised another group of younger scholars. A degree of uniformity for the three parts, however, was supplied by Harry M. Orlinsky of Hebrew Union College, who served as editor-in-chief throughout the project.[1]

The style of the rendering is at a high literary level, using a large vocabulary. The translators sought to determine as accurately as possible the meaning of the Hebrew and then to state the meaning in good contemporary English. In handling the sacred ineffable name, *YHWH,* the New Jewish Version has followed the long-established synagogue custom of rendering it as Lord. After the first edition of the first two volumes had appeared, some changes were made, which, while important in themselves, did little to alter in any substantial way the nature of the final text. For example, in the 1962 edition of *The Torah,* Genesis 1:26 reads "I will make man in My image, after My likeness," while the final edition reads "Let us make man in our image, after our likeness." Likewise, the first edition's "Let me, then, go down and confound their speech there" (Gen. 11:7) has been changed in the second edition to "Let us. . . ."

In 1999, the Jewish Publication Society issued the *JPS Hebrew-English Tanakh,* a diglot edition for the use of students. An engag-

---

1. Orlinsky also prepared a supplementary volume entitled *Notes on the New Translation of the Torah* (Philadelphia: Jewish Publication Society of America, 1969).

ing and efficient layout of two columns on each page enables the reader to move rapidly from one language to the other.

Despite the many resources available for the study of the original Hebrew and Aramaic texts and their interpretation, there still remain passages where the text and its meaning are unclear. The reader may be surprised to find that the footnote, "Meaning of Hebrew obscure" or its equivalent, occurs some 190 times in the translation of the Writings. This is especially true of the poetic books. One can almost feel the despair of the translators when at Job 24:18 they provide the note, "From here to the end of the chapter [verse 25] the translation is largely conjectural." One may hope that future discoveries and research will result in a clearer understanding of the meaning of obscure passages.

Heinz W. Cassirer's New Testament (1989)

Cassirer's translation of the New Testament, edited by Ronald Weitzman, who also supplied the introduction, is the work of a German-born Jew. In 1934, at the age of thirty-one, he came to Great Britain, where for many years he taught philosophy at the University of Glasgow and at Corpus Christi, Oxford. He was a scholar of wide-ranging interests and produced a study of Aristotle's *De anima,* commentaries on two of Kant's *Critiques,* and a book entitled *Grace and Law: St. Paul, Kant, and the Hebrew Prophets.* In 1955 he was baptized into the Anglican Church and soon afterwards brought his Jewish background and knowledge of Greek to bear on texts of the New Testament, beginning with the letters of the apostle Paul.

The translation itself sprang from Cassirer's own need for personal clarity and, in this respect, is noteworthy as a testimony to the impact of the New Testament on a mature academic of Jewish heritage who turned to biblical literature for answers to pressing philosophical questions, such as that of moral freedom. The title of Cassirer's translation is *God's New Covenant: A New Testament Translation* (Grand Rapids: Eerdmans, 1989). The leading blurb on the inside of the dust jacket states:

> This distinctive translation is the work of a Jewish classicist and philosopher who had not read a word of the Bible before the age of forty-nine. So great was the impact of the Greek biblical texts on Heinz Cassirer that he devoted the next twenty-one years of his life

This is clearly worth investigating

to studying them. . . . It [the translation] will be particularly rele-
vant to Christians wanting a deeper understanding of their own
spiritual roots as well to Jews interested in Christianity. . . . [It]
will be especially accessible to any who may be coming to these biblical texts for the first time.

The translation was eventually edited for publication by
Ronald Weitzman, who served as Cassirer's secretary during the
long process of translating. He tells us ("Introducing the Translation and Its Translator," pp. xvi–xvii) that "Cassirer showed no
desire to see this translation published in his lifetime. He expressed confidence that it would have its day, and was content to
say, 'Now it is up to the Holy Spirit.' He then made preparations
to begin translating Kant's major ethical work, *The Critique of
Practical Reason*."

The rendering of John 1:1–2, 14 is altogether solemn and
stately: "It was the Word that was at the very beginning; and the
Word was by the side of God, and the Word was the very same as
God. It was he who at the very beginning was by the side of God.
. . . So the Word became a creature of flesh and blood and made
his stay in our midst. And we saw his glory, the glory which is his
as the Father's only Son, coming forth from the Father, full of
grace and truth."

A much more expansive translation that conveys the meaning
admirably is the twenty-two English words that Cassirer used to
render Mark's five words in Greek, *baptisma metanoias eis aphesin
hamartiōn* (1:4): "a baptism which was to have its source in repentance and which was to result in people having their sins forgiven
them."

On the whole, however, the style of the translation leaves
something to be desired in the matter of consistency. Hours are
sometimes given in modern terms, but in other passages are third,
sixth, and ninth hour. Distances are sometimes in yards and miles
but elsewhere in furlongs. *Parabolē* may be "parable," "simile," or
"a figurative saying." The erroneous use of the reflexive for the
nominative is very common. Statements adverse to their prede-
cessor begin with "no" ("No, the Lord himself . . ."). Revelation
11:10 is not a complete sentence, and Luke 11:32 erroneously includes the word "not."

Despite such infelicities, it is to be hoped that the translation will be helpful to readers who fall into any of the three categories for whom the publisher claims the work has merit.

David H. Stern's Complete Jewish Bible (1998)

According to information provided on the last page of the book,

> David H. Stern was born in Los Angeles in 1935, the great-grandson of two of the city's first twenty Jews. He earned a Ph.D. in economics at Princeton University and was a professor at UCLA, mountain-climber, co-author of a book on surfing, and owner of health-food stores.
>
> In 1972 he came to faith in Yeshua as the Messiah, after which he received a Master of Divinity degree at Fuller Theological Seminary and did graduate work at the University of Judaism. . . .
>
> In 1979 the Stern family made *aliyah* (immigrated to Israel), where they live with their two children and are active in Israel's Messianic Jewish community. . . .

Dr. Stern's translation of the New Testament, entitled the *Jewish New Testament,* was published in 1989 by Jewish New Testament Publications.[2] The subtitle of the book succinctly states its purpose: "A translation of the New Testament that expresses its Jewishness." One of the ways it does this is by providing a transliteration of several key words and phrases, all of which are explained in footnotes on the pages where they occur, as well as in the "Pronouncing Explanatory Glossary" at the end of the volume (pp. 358–78). There are 356 entries in the glossary, of which 279 are proper nouns (personal and place names), and only 77 are common nouns and phrases. The transliteration of some of the proper names is quite needless: "A • **dam**" is Adam, "Ar • **ni**" is Arni, "Da • **vid**" is David, and so forth. Some are not so obvious: "Yᵊhu • **dah**" is Judah, "Yitz • **chak**" is Isaac, and "Ye • **shu** • a" is Jesus.

In 1998 Stern issued through Jewish New Testament Publications his *Complete Jewish Bible.* For the Old Testament, he adopted and adapted the 1917 translation issued by the Jewish Publication Society of America (see above). Its somewhat archaic English style

2. P.O. Box 1313 [later, P.O. Box 615], Clarksville, MD 21029.

was modified to agree with the translation in his *Jewish New Testament*. Occasionally, when Stern questioned the rendering of the Hebrew in the JPS's version, he translated the Hebrew of the Masoretic text himself. Consequently, his version of the Old Testament is something between a translation and a paraphrase.

The books of the Old Testament, of course, stand in the order of the Masoretic text. For the same reason, the initial descriptive phrase beginning many of the Psalms is numbered as verse 1. What is numbered verse 1 in other Bibles is verse 2 in Stern's text.

The following are several examples in Stern's version. (Italicized words are explained in the glossary.)

> ²God spoke to Moshe: he said to him, "I am *ADONAI*. ³I appeared to Avraham, Yitz'chak and Ya'akov as *El Shaddai*, although I did not make myself known to them by my name, *Yud-Heh-Vav-Heh* [*ADONAI*]. ⁴Also with them I established my covenant to give them the land of Kena'an, the land where they wandered about and lived as foreigners. (*Sh'mot* [Exodus] 6:2–4)

> The words of 'Amos, one of the sheep owners in T'koa, which he saw concerning Isra'el in the days of 'Uziyah king of Y'hudah and Yarov'am the son of Yo'ash, king of Isra'el, two years before the earthquake. (*'Amos* [Amos] 1:1)

> ¹When Yeshua learned that the *P'rushim* had heard he was making and immersing more *talmidim* than Yochanan ²(although it was not Yeshua himself who immersed but his *talmidim*), ³Yeshua left Y'hudah and set out again for the Galil. ⁴This meant that he had to pass through Shomron. (*Yochanan* [John] 4:1–4)

> ¹¹And now, brothers, *shalom*! Put yourselves in order, pay attention to my advice, be of one mind, live in *shalom*—and the God of love and *shalom* will be with you.
>   ¹²Greet one another with a holy kiss.
>   ¹³All God's people send greetings to you.
>   ¹⁴The grace of the Lord Yeshua the Messiah,
>   the love of God
>   and the fellowship of the *Ruach HaKodesh* be with you all.
>   (2 Corinthians 13:11–14)

In addition to transliterating various Hebrew words, Stern rather unexpectedly also includes the transliteration of ten or a dozen Yiddish words.[3] For example, in Luke 18:4–5 when the determined widow perseveres in her argument to the judge, he says to himself, "I don't fear God, and I don't respect other people; but because this widow is such a *nudnik*, I will see to it that she gets justice—otherwise, she'll keep coming and pestering me till she wears me out!" The context clearly indicates that the meaning is something like "pest" or "bore." In 1 Timothy 4:7, the neophyte pastor is advised to "refuse godless *bubbe-meises*." The glossary tells the non-Yiddish reader that this means "old wives' tales"; literally, "grandmothers' stories." The Seventy disciples (*talmidim*) are sent out with the admonition, "Don't carry a money-belt or a pack, and don't stop to *shmoose* with people on the road" (Luke 10:4). The glossary informs the reader that *shmoose* means "engage in friendly gossipy chit-chat."

An interesting typographical innovation is the use of a dramatic change in the type font when the translator wishes to show a change in the actual writer. A script font is used in 1 Corinthians 16:21–24, Galatians 6:11–18, Colossians 4:18, 2 Thessalonians 3:17–18, and Philemon 19a to indicate that Paul himself took the pen in hand to write the words presented in this way.

All in all, Stern's *Complete Jewish Bible* will certainly give the Gentile Christian reader a new perspective. It may be hoped that it will also be appreciated by its target audience, those who refer to themselves as Messianic Jews.

---

3. In a letter (7 September 2000) to the present writer, Stern explains, "I used [Yiddish expressions] in order to add a little 'ethnic spice' to my version, since one of my stated purposes was to demonstrate to Jews, Christians, and everyone else that the New Testament is a Jewish book."

fourteen

—

Revision after Revision

During the last decade and a half of the twentieth century, several English versions that had been published during the second half of that century underwent further revision. Some of the revisions were called for because of the discovery of more ancient Hebrew and Greek manuscripts; others were produced in the interest of improving the style of the English translation. *Keep up to current language of today*

The New American Standard Bible (1971; updated ed. 1995)

In 1959 the Lockman Foundation of La Habra, California (a nonprofit Christian corporation formed in 1942 to promote Christian education, evangelism, and, above all, Bible translation in several languages), launched a new translation project, based on the American Standard Version of 1901. Since the copyright of the ASV had expired, the Lockman Foundation was free to use and modify the text.

In 1971 the work of fifty-eight anonymous translators from a wide variety of denominational backgrounds was published as the New American Standard Bible. The revisers reverted to the traditional format of the Geneva Bible (1560) and the King James Bible (1611), in which each verse begins a new paragraph. Unlike the ASV, which uses Jehovah as the personal name of God (see p. 103 above), the traditional rendering of the Tetragrammaton was adopted, printed with capital letters (LORD).

An innovation introduced by the revisers was to print Old Testament quotations in the New Testament entirely in smaller capital letters. They also inserted quotation marks (the ASV did not use them), repeating them when necessary at the start of each successive verse. Paragraphs are designated by the use of boldface numbers or letters. "Thou," "Thee," and "Thy" are used only in prayer to the Deity. Contrary to the usage of scribes of biblical manuscripts, as well as the practice of almost all translators of the English Bible (including the ASV), the revisers capitalized all personal pronouns when referring to God, Jesus Christ, and the Holy Spirit.

Although the revisers of the NASB claim to have followed in most instances the text of the twenty-third edition of the Nestle Greek New Testament, important deviations occur in the introduction of a number of verses that rest on doubtful manuscript authority. These include Matthew 6:13b; 12:47; 18:11; 23:14; Mark 7:16; 9:44, 46; 11:26; 15:28; Luke 24:12; etc.

In 1995 an updated edition of the New American Standard Bible was issued (NASBU). It is said to rest in most instances upon the twenty-sixth edition of the Nestle Greek New Testament, but the previously mentioned deviations still occur in the updated edition. A considerable number of small translational changes have been made. According to a detailed analysis comparing the NASB and the NASBU,[1] the former contains 781,182 words and the latter 774,216 words. Changes introduced by the NASBU occur in 10,616 verses and directly affect 24,338 words in the NASB. There are only 4,704

---

1. Laurence M. Vance, *Double Jeopardy: The New American Standard Bible Update* (Vance Publications, P.O. Box 11781, Pensacola, FL 32524), published in 1998. Dr. Vance also supplies the names of the translators of the NASB and NASBU (pp. 299–300).

changes in capitalization, 32 in spelling, and 30 in italics. This makes 19,572 corrections involving word omissions, additions, transpositions, or substitutions in the text of the NASB. The updated edition makes about 85 changes that introduce gender-inclusive language.

The New Jerusalem Bible (1985)

Neither time nor biblical studies stand still, and a new edition of the *Bible de Jérusalem* appeared in 1973, making it necessary to prepare a new English edition as well. The New Jerusalem Bible (1985) is not just a translation of the French, but an edition in its own right, with textual improvement and explanatory notes, under the direction of the new editor, Dom Henry Wansborough of Ampleforth Abbey in Yorkshire.

Besides correcting defects in the 1966 edition, attention was given to the reduction of masculine-oriented language in passages that clearly involve both men and women. The editor points out in the foreword that "considerable efforts have been made, though not at all costs, to soften or avoid the inbuilt preference of the English language, a preference now found so offensive by some people, for the masculine; the word of the Lord concerns men and women equally."

Various changes avoid the use of what was seen as masculine bias: "Men of good omen" becomes "an omen of things to come" (Zech. 3:8), "the rich" (Mic. 6:12) displaces "rich men," "someone" (Zech. 4:1) and "everyone" (11:6) avoid the use of "man." "He who" (Amos 9:1) becomes "whoever." "The wicked man's oracle is sin" (Ps. 36:1) is now rendered "Sin is the oracle of the wicked."

The original Jerusalem Bible set out to discard all Bible English and adopted modern English usage. Several of these changes came under heavy criticism, and these are now amended. Thus, for example, in the Beatitudes (Matt. 5:3–11), "blessed" has been restored where JB had "happy." The rendering of the Greek *amēn, amēn legō hymin* as "I tell you most solemnly" (for example, John 16:20), also much criticized, has been altered to "In all truth I tell you." In 1 John 3:21 and 4:1 and 7, "My dear people" has been replaced by "My dear friends."

Revised New Testament, New American Bible (1986)

In 1978, only eight years after the publication of the New American Bible, plans were drawn up for a thorough revision of the New Testament. For this purpose, a steering committee was formed to organize and direct the work of revision, select collaborators, and serve as an editorial board to coordinate the work of the various revisers, as well as to determine the final form of the text and the explanatory materials. From December 1980 through September 1986, the editorial board met a total of fifty times to review and revise all of the material in order to ensure accuracy and consistency of approach. The editors also worked together with the bishops' ad hoc committee that had been appointed by the National Conference of Catholic Bishops in 1982 to oversee the revision.

In the preface to the revised edition of the New Testament, the translators acknowledge that

> Although the Scriptures are themselves timeless, translations and explanations of them quickly become dated in an era marked by rapid cultural change to a degree never experienced. The explosion of biblical studies that has taken place in our century and the changing nature of our language itself requires periodic adjustment both in translations and in the accompanying explanatory materials. The experience of actual use of the New Testament of *The New American Bible*, especially in oral proclamation, has provided a basis for further improvements. Accordingly, it was decided in 1978 to proceed with a thorough revision of the New Testament to reflect advances in scholarship and to satisfy needs identified through pastoral experience.

Since the primary aim of the revision was to produce a version as accurate and faithful to the meaning of the Greek original as is possible for a translation, the editors moved in the direction of a formal-equivalence approach. Happily, the translators acknowledge that "in passages where a particular Greek term retains the same meaning, it has been rendered in the same way insofar as this has been feasible. . . . The synoptic gospels have been carefully translated so as to reveal both the similarities and the differences of the Greek."

In other words, the disparate renderings mentioned in chapter 10 have now been amended.

Furthermore, where the meaning of the original is inclusive of both sexes, the translators have sought "to reproduce such inclusivity as far as this is possible in normal English usage without resort to inelegant circumlocutions or neologisms that would offend against the dignity of the languages." For example, the change at Matthew 23:13 from "You shut the doors of the kingdom of God in men's faces," to "You lock the kingdom of heaven before human beings," apart from being a more literal translation, reflects accommodation to gender-neutral language insofar as fidelity to the original allows. In short, the revised edition is a substantial improvement over the previous edition.

The Revised English Bible (1989)

Soon after the publication in 1970 of the New English Bible, a committee was formed to collect and assess criticism of the new translation. The minor revision of the version that was expected to result from the work of this committee turned out to be a significant major revision.[2] Professor W. D. McHardy, who served from 1968 as deputy director of the New English Bible, was appointed director of the revision. Although the NEB was sponsored by the main British churches, Roman Catholic representatives had attended only as observers. For the work of the revision, they joined as full members, as did also scholars of the Salvation Army and the Moravian Church. Thus, the REB is even more representative of British Christendom than the NEB.

From the companion book prepared by Roger Coleman, who worked as a coordinating editor for the project and as secretary to the supervising joint committee of the churches, we learn that there were nineteen revisers and twelve literary revisers. "By the time that the last of the confirmed copy was ready for the copy editor in November 1988, the revision process had been in train for fourteen years and two months."[3]

2. See Roger Coleman, *New Light and Truth: The Making of the Revised English Bible* (London: Oxford University Press and Cambridge University Press, 1989).
3. Coleman, *New Light and Truth*, p. 42.

Among his comments in the preface on the intentions of the reviewers, Dr. Donald Coggan (previously archbishop of Canterbury) mentions their care to ensure that

> The style of English used is fluent and of appropriate dignity for liturgical use, while maintaining intelligibility for worshippers of a wide range of ages and backgrounds. . . . As the "you"-form of address to God is now commonly used, the "thou"-form which was preserved in the language of prayer in The New English Bible has been abandoned. The use of male-oriented language, in passages of traditional versions of the Bible which evidently apply to both genders, has become a sensitive issue in recent years; the revisers have preferred more inclusive gender reference where that has been possible without compromising scholarly integrity or English style. (pp. viii–ix)

Some of the changes in wording are in the direction of a more conservative and less idiosyncratic rendering. For example, in speaking of Achsah (Josh. 15:18), instead of "she broke wind," the revisers say "she dismounted." Instead of "all men's knees run with urine" (Ezek. 21:7), the text now reads "all knees will turn to water." Paul's advice "Have nothing to do with loose livers" (1 Cor. 5:9) now becomes "Have nothing to do with those who are sexually immoral." On the other hand, no change was made in Proverbs 19:29, "There is a rod in pickle for the arrogant," or in Song of Songs 1:7, "That I [the bride] may not be left picking lice as I sit among your companions' herds," or Acts 1:21, "those who bore us company."

It is curious that in their rendering of the Ten Commandments, in addition to the presence of many small differences in the Hebrew text between Exodus 20 and Deuteronomy 5, as well as the major difference in the motivation for keeping the Sabbath, the revisers have introduced many more, even where the Hebrew wording is identical. For example, the introductory verse in Exodus reads, "I am the Lord your God who brought you out of the land of Egypt, out of the land of slavery," while in Deuteronomy we find, "I am the Lord your God who brought you out of Egypt, out of that land where you lived as slaves." Other examples include "You must have no other god [sing.] besides me" and "You must have no other gods [pl.] beside me" (with marginal alternatives in each case). Again, "You must not make a carved image for yourself" and "You are not to make . . . ." Yet again, "You must not bow down to them in worship" and "You must not worship or serve them." All these were appropriately rendered in the NEB.

One of the most puzzling features of the NEB was its translation of *ekklēsia* in Acts and the Epistles. In Acts, all local bodies outside Jerusalem were "congregations"; only the Jerusalem body was a "church." In the Epistles "church" referred only to the institution; all local bodies were "congregation(s)," "community," or "the meeting" (1 Cor. 14:23, 24).

The REB, on the other hand, has relaxed the distinction introduced in the NEB. In Acts, the Jerusalem body is always "church" (compare also "the church in Judaea" in 11:1), but other bodies are sometimes "church" and sometimes "congregation." The one at Antioch is both: "church" in 11:26; 13:1; 15:3, and "congregation" in 14:27. There are "churches" in Lystra and Iconium (16:5), but there is a mention of "(each) congregation" in Lystra, Iconium, and Pisidian Antioch (14:23). In Syria and Cilicia (15:41) and in Ephesus (20:17), REB has "churches."

It is good to find that in the Old Testament the headings of the Psalms have been restored. They are, after all, part of the Masoretic text, and it is odd that they were omitted in the NEB. The indications of the speakers in the Song of Songs have been retained from the NEB, but without stating that they come from two manuscripts of the Septuagint, as the original did.

In the New Testament, John 7:53–8:11 continues to be printed as a separate document at the end of John. The two endings of Mark have been reversed: REB has the shorter ending first, without a verse number and without any space between it and the close of verse 8, so that the average reader will assume it to be part of verse 8. The longer ending is separated from the shorter ending by an extra space, and the traditional verse numbers 9–20 are included. Footnotes explain the textual evidence.

Feb. 13, 2013

The New Revised Standard Version (1990)

In light of the discovery of further fragments of the Dead Sea Scrolls of the Old Testament and further early Greek papyrus manuscripts of the New Testament, in 1974 the National Council of Churches directed that the Standard Bible Committee undertake a thorough revision of the RSV (1952) in accordance with the following mandates.[4] Necessary changes were to be made (1) in paragraph structure and punctuation; (2) in the elimination of archaisms while retaining the flavor of the Tyndale–King James Bible tradition; (3) in attaining greater accuracy, clarity, and euphony; and (4) in eliminating masculine-oriented language concerning people, so far as this could be done without distorting passages that reflect the historical situation of ancient patriarchal culture and society.

Thereafter, the Standard Bible Committee was convened twice every year, usually one week in January and one week in June. Its members, unlike those of some other revision committees, continued to contribute their time and expertise to the project without financial remuneration. Eventually, several additional members were added to the Old Testament section (making a total of twenty members) so that three subsections could meet simultaneously and thus keep up with the ten-member panel that was working on the New Testament and the books of the Apocrypha. As vice-chairs, Robert Denton and Walter Harrelson, along with one or another member of the Old Testament section, served as conveners of the three Old Testament subsections. As chair of the Standard Bible Committee, the present writer served as convener of the New Testament section and the section for the Apocrypha, which met in alternate seasons.

The work of revision, which had involved face-to-face discussion from 9:00 A.M. to 9:00 P.M. (with time off for meals, where discussion was often resumed), was at length finished, and on May 16, 1990, at the Episcopal Cathedral in Pittsburgh, the National Council of Churches held a service of blessing and commemoration of the New Revised Standard Version of the Bible.

Seven publishers in the United States and in Great Britain were licensed to issue the new version. Within a few years, the NRSV was available in more than seventy different sizes, formats, and bindings, with a variety of maps, illustrations, and annotations.

Examples of significant changes made in revising the RSV include the following:

---

4. See Bruce M. Metzger, Robert C. Dentan, and Walter Harrelson, *The Making of the New Revised Standard Version of the Bible* (Grand Rapids: Eerdmans, 1991).

1. Greater Accuracy

	RSV	NRSV
Amos 6:5	like David invent for themselves instruments of music	like David improvise on instruments of music
Luke 7:47	[H]er sins, which are many, are forgiven, for she loved much.	[H]er sins, which were many, have been forgiven; hence she has shown great love.
John 2:15	And making a whip of cords, he drove them all, with the sheep and oxen, out of the temple.	Making a whip of cords, he drove all of them out of the temple, both the sheep and the cattle.

2. Improved Clarity

	RSV	NRSV
Exod. 11:8	And he [Moses] went out from Pharaoh in hot anger.	And in hot anger he left Pharaoh.
1 Sam. 11:2	gouge out all your right eyes	gouge out everyone's right eye
Mic. 1:11	[T]he wailing of Beth-ezel shall take away from you its standing place.	Beth-ezel is wailing and shall remove its support from you.
Zech. 3:3	Now Joshua was standing before the angel, clothed in filthy garments.	Now Joshua was dressed with filthy clothes as he stood before the angel.

3. More Intelligible English

	RSV	NRSV
Ps. 86:11	[U]nite my heart to fear thy name.	[G]ive me an undivided heart to revere your name.

	RSV	NRSV
2 Cor. 6:11	Our mouth is open to you, Corinthians; our heart is wide.	We have spoken frankly to you Corinthians; our heart is wide open to you.
2 Cor. 7:2	Open your hearts to us.	Make room in your hearts for us.

4. More Natural English

	RSV	NRSV
Deut. 29:5	[Y]our sandals have not worn off your feet.	[T]he sandals on your feet have not worn out.
1 Sam. 24:11	though you hunt my life to take it	though you are hunting me to take my life
Ps. 98:8	[L]et the hills sing for joy together.	[L]et the hills sing together for joy.
Matt. 12:34	[H]ow can you speak good, when you are evil?	How can you speak good things, when you are evil?
Acts 12:6	The very night when Herod was about to bring him out, Peter was sleeping between two soldiers, bound with two chains.	The very night before Herod was going to bring him out, Peter, bound with two chains, was sleeping between two soldiers.
Heb. 11:16	[God] has prepared for them a city.	[God] has prepared a city for them.

5. Adjustments of Renderings That Could Be Misunderstood

	RSV	NRSV
1 Kings 19:21	Then he arose and went after Elijah.	Then he set out and followed Elijah.

	RSV	NRSV
Ps. 39:9	I am dumb.	I am silent.
Ps. 50:9	I will accept no bull from your house.	I will not accept a bull from your house.
Ps. 119:86	All thy commandments are sure; they persecute me with falsehood.	All your commandments are enduring; I am persecuted without cause.
2 Cor. 11:25	[O]nce I was stoned.	Once I received a stoning.

6. Avoidance of Ambiguity in Oral Reading

	RSV	NRSV
Gen. 35:7	because there God had revealed himself	because it was there that God had revealed himself
Ps. 122:5	There thrones for judgment were set.	For there the thrones for judgment were set up.
Luke 22:35	"[D]id you lack anything?" They said, "Nothing."	"[D]id you lack anything?" They said, "No, not a thing."

7. Better Euphony

	RSV	NRSV
Isa. 6:2	[W]ith two he flew [often misheard as *tui flu*].	[W]ith two they flew.
Isa. 22:16	[Y]ou have hewn here a tomb for yourself, you who hew a tomb on the height.	[Y]ou have cut out a tomb here for yourself, cutting a tomb on the height.
Luke 19:32	So those who were sent went away.	So those who were sent departed.

8. Elimination of "Man" or "Men" When Neither Occurs in the Original Text

	RSV	NRSV
Matt. 6:30	O men of little faith	you of little faith
John 2:10	Every man serves the good wine first; and when men have drunk freely, then the poor wine.	Everyone serves the good wine first, and then the inferior wine after the guests have become drunk.
John 12:32	[A]nd I, when I am lifted up from the earth, will draw all men to myself.	And I, when I am lifted up from the earth, will draw all people to myself.
Rom. 16:7	[Andronicus and Junias] are men of note among the apostles.	[Andronicus and Junia] are prominent among the apostles.

9. Elimination of Unnecessary Masculine Renderings

	RSV	NRSV
Matt. 4:4	Man shall not live by bread alone.	One does not live by bread alone.
Luke 6:45	The good man out of the good treasure of his heart produces good, and the evil man out of the evil treasure produces evil.	The good person out of the good treasure of the heart produces good, and the evil person out of evil treasure produces evil.
Gal. 6:6	Let him who is taught the word share all good things with him who teaches.	Those who are taught the word must share in all good things with their teacher.
2 Cor. 10:17	Let him who boasts, boast of the Lord.	Let the one who boasts, boast in the Lord.

	RSV	NRSV
Eph. 3:16	grant you to be strengthened with might through his Spirit in the inner man	grant that you may be strengthened in your inner being with power through his Spirit
Eph. 4:28	Let the thief no longer steal, but rather let him labor, doing honest work with his hands.	Thieves must give up stealing; rather let them labor and work honestly with their own hands.
Rev. 2:29	He who has an ear, let him hear what the Spirit says to the churches.	Let anyone who has an ear listen to what the Spirit is saying to the churches.

No gender changes were made in language pertaining to the Deity.

The New Revised Standard Version continues to be (with the RSV) the most ecumenical of all English versions of the Scriptures. It contains not only the sixty-six books of the Protestant canon of the Old and the New Testaments but also all the books accepted by Roman Catholic, Eastern Orthodox, and Slavonic Churches. The Common Bible issued by Thomas Nelson Publishers in 1991 identifies in the table of contents the four groupings of the apocryphal/deuterocanonical books: (1) books and additions to Esther and Daniel in Roman Catholic, Greek, and Slavonic Bibles; (2) books in Greek and Slavonic Bibles but not in the Roman Catholic canon; (3) books in the Slavonic Bible and in the Latin Vulgate appendix; (4) books in an appendix to the Greek Bible.

In order to make the rendering of the NRSV Bible still more acceptable in Great Britain and the Commonwealth nations, in 1994 Nigel Lynn of Oxford University Press was granted permission to produce an anglicized edition. This involved the introduction of British spelling, grammar, and punctuation (single quotation marks instead of double), as well as the adoption of a limited number of changes in wording in order to replace Americanisms with expressions more usual to British readers. For the preparation of the copy embodying such modifications, the press secured the services of Roger Coleman, who had been in charge of the editorial administration and coordination of the work that resulted in the Revised English Bible (1989). The anglicized edition of the NRSV was issued in the autumn of 1995.

Examples of changes in wording (all of which needed the approval of the chair of the Standard Bible Committee) included "cornfields" instead of "grainfields" (Matt. 12:1), "stock of Jesse" instead of "stump of Jesse" (Isa. 11:1), and "angels mounted on horses" instead of "angels on horseback" (4 Macc. 4:10). In the case of the passage in 4 Maccabees, it was difficult for an American to appreciate the need for any change at all until Coleman pointed out that the *Oxford Dictionary of Current English* defines "angels-on-horseback" as a culinary term meaning "savoury of oysters wrapped in slices of bacon"!

In 1999 Oxford University Press issued *The Common Worship Lectionary*, a volume of more than twelve hundred pages that presents the Scripture lessons for Sundays and principal feasts and holy days from the anglicized edition of the New Revised Standard Version, which, according to the statement of Bishop Kenneth Stevenson in the preface, "is gaining widespread acceptance in churches today." In fact, even prior to the publication of the anglicized edition, the Faculty of Divinity at Cambridge University voted to adopt the NRSV Bible as the recommended English version for use in the undergraduate courses of religion at the university. Similar decisions were made at other British universities and colleges.

fifteen

Simplified, Easy-to-Read Versions

The Basic English Bible (1949)

This version of the Bible is intended to bring the English Bible, in a form easily understood, to the many potential readers all over the world who know only a little English. Basic English is a simplified form of English devised by the British semasiologist C. K. Ogden of Cambridge University. It comprises a vocabulary of 850 words, which, when used in accordance with a few simple rules, can express the meaning of everything that can be said in English. It can be learned in a fraction of the time it takes to learn a second language, and it can, of course, be understood by everyone who already knows English. Very often, it cannot be distinguished from everyday English.

Shortly before the outbreak of the Second World War, the Orthological Institute of Cambridge arranged for Professor S. H.

Hooke[1] of the University of London to undertake the production of a Basic English version of the Bible. The New Testament was published in 1941 and the whole Bible in 1949. By the addition of fifty special "Bible" words (e.g., "cubit," "gopher" wood), together with a further hundred words listed as giving most help in reading English poetic verse, the available vocabulary was raised from 850 to 1,000.

Basic English is remarkably deficient in verbs (it has fewer than twenty). Nevertheless, this handicap was largely overcome by the genius of Professor Hooke, who, with the collaboration of Mrs. Hooke as his sole collaborator, did not turn any existing version of the English Bible into Basic English but produced an independent rendering from the original languages.

The capacity of Basic English to reproduce biblical text may be illustrated by the Twenty-third Psalm:

> The Lord takes care of us as his sheep; I will not be without any good thing. He makes a resting-place for me in the green fields: he is my guide by the quiet waters. He gives new life to my soul: he is my guide in the ways of righteousness because of his name. Yes, though I go through the valley of deep shade, I will have no fear of evil; for you are with me, your rod and your support are my comfort. You make ready a table for me in front of my haters: you put oil on my head; my cup is overflowing. Truly, blessing and mercy will be with me all the days of my life; and I will have a place in the house of the Lord all my days.

J. B. Phillips's Version (1958; rev. ed. 1972)

It was in 1941, during the Second World War and amid the London blitz, that an Anglican parish minister of scholarly bent began a new translation of the New Testament. While seated in an air raid shelter, J. B. Phillips, vicar of the Church of the Good Shepherd in London, worked at a fresh rendering of the twenty-one epistles of the New Testament. He chose to begin with the epistles because he considered them to "provide that spiritual vitamin, without which human life is at best sickly, and at most

---

1. For "A Personal Appreciation" of Professor Hooke on his ninetieth birthday, see the Very Rev. W. R. Matthew's contribution to Hooke's Festschrift in *Promise and Fulfilment*, ed. F. F. Bruce (Edinburgh: Clark, 1963), pp. 1–6.

dead." This first installment, entitled *Letters to Young Churches: A Translation of the New Testament Epistles,* was published in 1947 by Geoffrey Bles of London and instantly became a best-seller. It was dedicated to the task of conveying to the modern reader the full import of the original in an easy-to-read style. To attain this end, the translator (according to Phillips) had to be "free to expand or explain" the text.

In the judgment of F. F. Bruce:

> Of all modern English translations of the New Testament epistles, this is one of the best—perhaps actually the best—for the ordinary reader. The reader who has never paid much attention to Paul's writings, and finds them dull and sometimes unintelligible in the older versions, would be well advised to read them through in Dr. Phillips's version. He will find them (possibly to his surprise) interesting and (more surprising still) remarkably relevant to the present day and its problems.[2]

Phillips continued his work on the other books of the New Testament. *The Gospels Translated into Modern English* was issued in 1952. In 1957, at the time of the twelfth printing of this rendering, Phillips indicated in the preface that "a thorough revision . . . has taken several months and I confess myself astonished at the large number of small corrections I have felt bound to make. The only excuse I have to offer is that the original work was done amid the busyness and pressure of parochial duties, and that until recently there has not been time for a word-by-word revision." In 1955 the Book of Acts was issued under the title *The Young Church in Action*; an appendix to the book gives Phillips's imaginative expansion of the sermons of Peter, Stephen, and Paul at Pentecost, Mars Hill, and so on.

Finally, in 1956 Phillips issued *The Book of Revelation: A New Translation of the Apocalypse.* He indicates in his preface that he had been tempted to omit this book altogether from his translational work—a course, incidentally, taken by Calvin in his New Testament Commentary. In the end, however, Phillips concluded that "although the task was not the same as it had been in the other

---

2. F. F. Bruce, *The English Bible: A History of Translations* (New York: Oxford University Press, 1970), p. 223.

parts of the New Testament, it could prove useful and even, in the true sense of that threadbare word, thrilling. For in this book the translator is carried into another dimension—he has but the slightest foothold in the time-and-space world with which he is familiar. He is carried, not into some never-never land of fancy, but into the ever-ever land of God's eternal Values and Judgments" (p. ix).

In 1958 the parts were collected together in one volume and published under the title of *The New Testament in Modern English.* One of the chief criticisms leveled against Phillips related to the Greek text underlying his rendering. Although he did not specify which edition of the Greek text he followed, it appears that in numerous passages he used the Textus Receptus rather than a critically established text, such as that of Westcott and Hort or Nestle.

Following the publication in 1966 of the United Bible Societies' new edition of the Greek New Testament, Phillips decided to undertake a thorough reexamination of his rendering. In addition to following the UBS Greek text, Phillips also removed many conversationally worded additions, like "as I am sure you realise" or "you must know now," and many extra words that do not occur in the Greek text at all. Nevertheless, at the close of five of the letters, in place of "Greet one another with a holy kiss" (Rom. 16:16; also 1 Cor. 16:20; 2 Cor. 13:12; 1 Thess. 5:26; 1 Pet. 5:14), Phillips has kept what he regarded as its modern equivalent, "Give each other a hearty handshake all round in Christian love."

Phillips's revised edition of *The New Testament in Modern English* (New York: Macmillan, 1972) continues to speak to the reader with verve and directness, as the following excerpt from Paul's Letter to Philemon will show:

> Although I could rely on my authority in Christ and dare to *order* you to do what I consider right, I am not doing that. No, I am appealing in love, a simple personal appeal from Paul the old man, in prison for Christ Jesus' sake. I am appealing for my child. Yes I have become a father though I have been under lock and key, and the child's name is—Onesimus! Oh, I know you have found him useless in the past but he is going to be useful now, to both of us. I am sending him back to you—part of my very heart. I should have dearly loved to have kept him with me: he could have done what you would have done—looked after me here in prison for the gospel's sake. But I would do nothing without consulting you first, for

if you have a favour to give me, let it be spontaneous and not forced
from you by circumstances!   2-20-13

The Good News Bible (Today's English Version) (1976)

The New Testament of the Good News Bible was issued on September 15, 1966, by the American Bible Society under the title *Good News for Modern Man.*[3] The idea of such a rendering arose in the following way. For a number of years, the American Bible Society had received requests from Africa and the Far East for a translation especially designed for those who speak English as an acquired language. Late in 1961, a secretary of a denominational board of home missions in America wrote to the society inquiring whether there was available a rendering that would be suitable for use among new literates and among foreign language groups in the United States.

As a result of such requests, the Bible Society decided that the time had come to prepare a common-language translation of the Scriptures in English. Robert G. Bratcher, a Baptist minister and missionary to Brazil, was invited to draw up initial drafts of the books of the New Testament. These were sent to translation consultants of the American Bible Society and to the translations department of the British and Foreign Bible Society. On the basis of their comments and suggestions, Bratcher introduced a variety of modifications in his rendering of the New Testament. After its publication in 1966, other comments and suggestions from readers started coming in. On the basis of these, on October 1, 1967, a second edition was published, incorporating many changes in both style and substance. As a result of its subsequent use in many parts of the world and of further comments received since then, a third edition was issued in 1973. Meanwhile, work had already been begun on the preparation of the Old Testament, and, with the assistance of several scholars, this was issued in 1976, along with a revised New Testament, under the title The Good News Bible (also called Today's English Version). The apocryphal/deuterocanonical books appeared in 1979.

3. See Eugene A. Nida, *Good News for Everyone: How to Use the Good News Bible* (Waco, Tex.: Word, 1977).

The 1976 edition of the Good News Bible endeavored to avoid male-oriented language, but a decade later it had become clear that further revision was advisable. In 1986 the American Bible Society's board of managers approved the undertaking of a new edition of both Testaments that would be more sensitive to issues of gender. It was published in 1992.

The Good News Bible is not a word-for-word translation. Instead, it adopts the principles of what Eugene A. Nida of the American Bible Society called "dynamic equivalence" or, more recently, "functional equivalence." Customs not known today are reworded; thus, "anointed my head with oil" (Ps. 23:5) becomes "welcomed me as an honored guest." The rendering avoids slang but uses colloquialisms of contemporary American speech, such as "She nagged him" (Judg. 14:17) and "You smart aleck, you" (1 Sam. 17:28).

Because the Good News Bible was designed to reach readers who were unfamiliar with traditional biblical language, adjustments in vocabulary were made. In 2 Samuel 7:16, instead of the literal "thy throne shall be established for ever," the GNB reads, "Your dynasty will never end." In Romans 12:20, "heap coals of fire on his head" (often read as abuse or torture) becomes "make him burn with shame." Psalm 23:3, "for his name's sake" (often misheard as "namesake"), becomes "as he had promised."[4]

The Reader's Digest Bible (1982)

For a good many years, the Reader's Digest Association had been publishing condensations of books generally considered to be classics. In the mid-1970s, the editors of the condensed books project gave serious consideration to the question of whether to issue a condensation of the Bible. On the one hand, they rightly regarded the Bible as a classic. On the other hand, however, they did not wish to alienate those among their customers who might consider it sacrilegious to condense the Holy Scriptures.

After becoming convinced that such a project would, on the whole, be welcomed, the Reader's Digest editors made inquiries

4. While the present book was passing through the press, the American Bible Society announced that, in North America, the Good News Bible (GNB) is to be renamed the Good News Translation (GNT).

among various persons as to which English version of the Bible should be chosen for condensation. Eventually, the Revised Standard Version (1952) was chosen as the basic text because of its wide usage, impeccable scholarship, and linkage to the King James Version, thus preserving the elevated and dignified tone cherished by so many generations of Bible readers.

In the course of time, I was invited to serve as general editor of the Reader's Digest Bible. My responsibilities were to advise which block cuts could be made in a given biblical book.[5] After the Digest's editors had eliminated unneeded words ("he answered and said" could be reduced by fifty percent to "he answered"), the general editor was to review their work and to discuss all points still at issue.

Unlike other "shorter Bibles," it was planned that this one would not omit any of its sixty-six books. The aim was to produce a text, shortened and clarified, yet preserving every incident, personality, and teaching of substance, while keeping the essence and flavor of the familiar language of Scripture.

The extent to which nonessential words were pruned from the text varied from book to book, and the amount of condensation of each book was determined by the character of the book itself. The final result was that the Old Testament was cut by about 50 percent, and the New Testament by about 25 percent. It was decided that some texts were not to be modified in any way, not even by the elimination of a single word. This list included the Ten Commandments, Psalm 23, the Beatitudes in Matthew 5, the Lord's Prayer, John 3:16, chapter 13 of 1 Corinthians, and others. As general editor, I insisted that when a transitional sentence was formed in order to link together two sections remaining after a block had been excised, no word or expression was to be used that did not belong to the vocabulary of the Revised Standard Version.

In September 1982, The Reader's Digest Bible, a volume of 767 pages with one column of text to a page, was published at Pleas-

5. For example, the seventh chapter of Numbers repeats twelve times an identical enumeration of the components of the daily offering made by the representative of each of the twelve tribes of Israel. Other passages, such as the genealogies in Genesis, 1 Chronicles, Ezra, Nehemiah, as well as many of the dietary laws in Leviticus were judged to be of reduced relevance in a condensed edition of the Scriptures.

antville, New York. One year later, a British edition entitled *The Reader's Bible* was published in London. It contained a foreword written by Dr. Donald Coggan, former archbishop of Canterbury. The popularity of the condensed Bible in English led to the publication of similar editions in other languages. In 1985 an Italian edition was issued (with the imprimatur), entitled *La Bibbia: Edizione condensata di selezione dal Reader's Digest.* Since it also contained condensations of the deuterocanonical books and was adorned with a good many pictures, some in color, the volume was considerably larger and heavier than the English version. A Korean version was published in 1987, and in 1990 a French illustrated edition was issued in Paris, and a British illustrated edition in London.

Among the numerous modern versions, one may ask, what place does the RDB have? That the RDB is not intended to replace the complete and uncondensed Bible is worthy of emphasis. It is designed to serve as a shortened, simplified, and easy-to-read summary of the contents of the entire biblical text.

The Contemporary English Version (1995)

Besides the Good News Bible mentioned above, the American Bible Society undertook the production of another modern speech translation, eventually named the Contemporary English Version.[6] At the start it was planned as a translation for early youth and focused on the vocabulary and understanding of children in grades one through three. Made directly from the original texts, it is not a paraphrase or modernization of any existing traditional version.

The work of translating was begun by Barclay M. Newman, who was joined later by Donald Johns and Steven Berneking. It continued under Newman's direction, with the editorial assistance of Jean Newman and the participation of over one hundred other translators, English language specialists, and biblical scholars. The aim of the project was to produce a version that could be

6. See Barclay M. Newman, Charles S. Houser, et al., *Creating and Crafting the Contemporary English Version: A New Approach to Bible Translation* (New York: American Bible Society, 1996).

understood more easily by readers and hearers than even the Good News Bible.

Since more people hear the Bible read than read it for themselves, Newman and his colleagues set themselves to listen carefully for how each word in their version would be perceived when read aloud. Theological terms, such as "justification," "sanctification," "righteousness," are replaced by other expressions or phrases appropriate to the context. "Story" is the preferred rendering for "parable," and "hooray" is used for "hosanna." Where both men and women are intended, gender-generic or inclusive language is employed. In the Gospel of John, where references to "the Jews" can be taken as anti-Semitic but only a certain segment of Judaism may be intended, phrases such as "the crowd" or "the leaders" are used so as to reduce the offensiveness.

The translators of the Contemporary English Version have developed a text with "measured" lines in poetic or rhythmic passages. For example:

> Did you ever tell the sun to rise?
>   And did it obey?
> Did it take hold of the earth
>   and shake out the wicked
>   like dust from a rug?
> Early dawn outlines the hills
>   like stitches on clothing
>   or sketches on clay.
> But its light is too much
>   for those who are evil,
>   and their power is broken. (Job 38:12–15)

> If we died with Christ, we will live with him.
>   If we don't give up, we will rule with him.
> If we deny that we know him,
>   he will deny that he knows us.
> If we are not faithful, he will still be faithful.
>   Christ cannot deny who he is. (2 Tim. 2:11–13)

New International Reader's Version (1996)

In August 1991, Zondervan Publishing House drew up guidelines for developing a simplified version at a reading level of third or fourth grade that was intended as a stepping stone to the New International Version. The board of the International Bible Society voted to begin the project early in 1992. In March of 1992, a committee met to establish working guidelines, some of which discussed policy on gender-inclusive language—a certain amount of which would be allowed. Forty translators and simplifiers of the edition were chosen from fourteen denominations. Many of the translators had also worked on the NIV. The initial simplification of all of the books of the Bible was completed in early 1994. In March of that year, the New Testament was completed, and the name New International Reader's Version was announced by the International Bible Society in August 1994. The Old Testament was completed by the end of 1995.

In November 1996, Hodder and Stoughton issued in Great Britain the simplified NIV under the title: *New International Version Popular Edition, Inclusive Language* and in March 1997 under the title *New International Version: Inclusive Language Edition* (NIVI). These cannot legally be sold in America.

Meanwhile, market research in America prompted Zondervan to proceed slowly. Some of Zondervan's clientele reacted violently against the idea that Zondervan might issue an inclusive-language edition.[7] Eventually, the decision was made that the simplified Bible could use a limited amount of gender-inclusive language (notably, in the Epistles *adelphoi* ["brothers"] could be rendered "brothers and sisters").

The preface to the New International Reader's Version (NIrV) issued by Zondervan (1996) describes the rendering as follows:

> The NIV is easy to understand and very clear. . . . We made the NIrV even easier to read and understand. We used the words of the NIV when we could. Sometimes we used shorter words. We explained words that might be hard to understand. We made the sentences shorter. . . . Sometimes the writers of the Bible used more than one name for the same person or place. For example, in the New Testament the Sea of Galilee is also called the Sea of Tiberias. But in the NIrV we decided to call it the Sea of Galilee everywhere it appears in the New Testament. . . . We also wanted to help our readers learn

7. For a balanced and clearheaded analysis of the brouhaha that erupted, see D. A. Carson, *The Inclusive Language Debate: A Plea for Realism* (Grand Rapids: Baker, 1998).

the names of people and places even in verses where those names don't actually appear. For example, when we knew that "the River" meant "the Euphrates River," we used these words even in verses where only the words "the River" are found.

The style of the NIrV (revised 1998), which contains some gender-inclusive language, can be evaluated from 1 Thessalonians 5:12–14:

Brothers and sisters, we ask you to have respect for the godly leaders who work hard among you. They have authority over you. They correct you. Have a lot of respect for them. Love them because of what they do. Live in peace with each other.

Brothers and sisters, we are asking you to warn those who don't want to work. Cheer up those who are shy. Help those who are weak. Put up with everyone.

Finally, several examples are given comparing the renderings of the NIV, NIVI, and NIrV (revised 1998).

Genesis 1:27
NIV   God created man in his own image.
NIVI   God created human beings in his likeness.
NIrV   God created man in his own likeness.

Psalm 1:1
NIV   Blessed is the man who does not walk in the counsel of the wicked.
NIVI   Blessed are those who do not walk in the counsel of the wicked.
NIrV   Blessed is the one who obeys the law of the Lord.

Proverbs 5:21
NIV   A man's ways are in full view of the Lord.
NIVI   Your ways are in full view of the Lord.
NIrV   The Lord watches a man's ways.

Luke 17:3
NIV   If your brother sins, rebuke him, and if he repents, forgive him.

NIVI Rebuke a brother or sister who sins, and if they repent, forgive them.

NIrV If your brother sins, tell him he is wrong. Then if he turns away from his sins, forgive him.

John 11:50

NIV   It is better for you that one man die for the people.

NIVI It is better for you that one person die for the people.

NIrV It is better for you if one man dies for the people.

Revelation 3:20

NIV   If anyone hears my voice and opens the door, I will come in and eat with him, and he with me.

NIVI If anyone hears my voice and opens the door, I will come in and eat with them and they with me.

NIrV If any of you hears my voice and opens the door, I will come in and eat with you. And you will eat with me.

sixteen

—

Paraphrases of the English Bible

The concise *Oxford Dictionary of Current English* defines *paraphrase* as "Free rendering or amplification of a passage, expression of its sense in other words."[1] The following are selected paraphrases of part or all of the English Bible.

Henry Hammond's *Paraphrase and Annotations* (1653)

The first noteworthy English paraphrase of the New Testament was compiled by Henry Hammond, an Anglican divine and scholar (1605–60). His *magnum opus,* a splendid achievement in English theological scholarship, was entitled *Paraphrase and Annotations upon all the Books of the New Testament, briefly Explaining all the*

---

1. Ed. Della Thompson, 2d ed. (Oxford and New York: Oxford University Press, 1993).

Difficult Places thereof (London, 1653). This pioneer work by "the father of English biblical criticism," was recommended by Dr. Johnson as the best commentary on the New Testament.[2] It went through numerous editions, the British Museum Catalogue listing the 1702 edition as the seventeenth edition. It finally appeared as a new edition (Oxford, 1845) in four volumes octavo.

On each page the Scripture text is given in the Authorized or King James Version with certain sections and phrases enclosed within square brackets. The paraphrase of the portions enclosed in brackets is given in a parallel column printed in smaller sized type. Following each chapter are learned discussions of exegetical and historical problems, often with extensive quotations of Greek, Hebrew, and Syriac sources, as well as numerous Greek and Latin patristic authors. At the end are two indexes, one of the Greek and the other of English words and phrases that are explained in the annotations.

Philip Doddridge's *Family Expositor* (1739–56)

Another widely used English paraphrase was prepared by an important Nonconformist divine and hymn writer, Philip Doddridge (1702–51). The twentieth child of his parents, so few were the signs of life at his birth that at first he was given up for dead. Despite having a frail constitution throughout life, Doddridge was among the pioneers of the modern missionary enterprise. Of his many writings, which comprise sermons, commentaries, devotional pieces, theological treatises, and a large number of hymns— many of which are still in use today—his best known work is *The Family Expositor, or, a Paraphrase and Version of the New Testament, with critical Notes and a practical Improvement*[3] *to each Section,* in six volumes (1739–56).

At the beginning of the first volume, Doddridge makes the following suggestions for reading the *Family Expositor*:

> As to the manner of reading this book in families, I would advise as follows:—First let the passage of Scripture be read from the *common*

2. James Boswell, *Life of Samuel Johnson* (London, 1791), 3:52 (anno 1776).
3. By "Improvement" Doddridge means what today is called "life application" of the passage.

translation [= the King James version] in the inner column, unless the family have their Bibles before them: then read the *New Family version* by itself, which is interwoven with the *Paraphrase*, but distinguished by the *Italic character*; and then the *Paraphrase* and *Improvement*. As for the *Notes*, I should advise the person who officiates, to select such as are of most general concern, and read them after the paragraph to which they belong: for it is not so agreeable to interrupt the sense to introduce them before it is completed.

For a time, paraphrases of Scripture fell out of general use, but in the twentieth century, several were published and have been widely used. Besides J. B. Phillips's version, which at various places introduces paraphrastic rendering, the following are quite consistently paraphrastic renderings.

F. F. Bruce's Expanded Paraphrase of the Epistles of Paul (1965)

In connection with a series of talks on the Pauline Letters, the Rylands Professor of Biblical Criticism and Exegesis in the University of Manchester, F. F. Bruce, prepared during the course of six years paraphrases covering the whole Pauline corpus. Published successively in *The Evangelical Quarterly,* these were subsequently revised and collected in one volume, called *An Expanded Paraphrase*, and published by the Postmaster Press of Exeter, England. An American edition was issued the same year by William B. Eerdmans Publishing Company of Grand Rapids, Michigan. When copies of these printings were exhausted, the volume was copyrighted in 1981 by the Paternoster Press, and the American edition was issued the same year by Ronald N. Haynes Publishers, Palm Springs, California.

For the convenience and interest of readers who may wish to make a literal rendering of the Greek text, Bruce's paraphrase is printed on pages facing the rendering of the Revised Version of 1881. This version is also equipped with the RV's expanded marginal cross-references produced for the Oxford and Cambridge University Presses by Dr. F. H. A. Scrivener and Professor W. F. Moulton and completed by Professor Moulton's former pupil, Dr. A. W. Greenup, and his son, Dr. J. H. Moulton.

As would be expected, Bruce's work is careful and scholarly. It deserves to be consulted by commentators on any of the Pauline Letters. Bruce comments in his introduction that while he has touched as lightly as possible on the critical problems of the Pauline corpus, "It may suffice to say here that the technique of translating or paraphrasing the three Pastoral Epistles has proved to be notably different from that which is called for by the other ten" (p. 12). As a sample of Bruce's style of paraphrasing, a portion of his work on Philemon may be cited corresponding to verses 4–14.

I always thank my God, Philemon, as I remember you in my prayers, for I hear good news of the love and loyalty which you show to our Lord Jesus and all His holy people. So I pray that your Christian liberality, springing as it does, from your faith, may lead you effectively into the experience and appreciation of every blessing which we have as fellow-members of Christ. Your love has brought me great joy and comfort, my dear brother; you have refreshed the hearts of God's people.

That is why I am making this request of you; I am making it for love's sake, although I could quite well exercise my authority in Christ's name and *command* you to do the proper thing. Yes, I could command you as Paul, ambassador[4] of Christ Jesus; but instead of that, I am now asking you a favour as Paul, *prisoner* of Christ Jesus. The request I am making is in behalf of my son. My son? Yes, my son. I have acquired him here in prison. His name is Onesimus—useful by name and useful by nature. I know that in former days you found him quite useless, but now, I assure you, he has learned to be true to his name—useful to you, and useful to me.

Well, I am sending him back to you, though it is like tearing out my very heart to do so. My own inclination is to keep him here with me, and then he could go on serving me while I am a prisoner for the gospel's sake—serving me as your representative. But I do not want to do anything without your consent; I do not want the good turn you are doing me through his service to be done by you willy-nilly, but in your free initiative.

4. Bruce adds a footnote: "Taking Gk *presbytēs* ('old man') in the sense of *presbeutēs* ('ambassador'). Cf. Eph. 6:20."

Kenneth Taylor's *Living Bible, Paraphrased* (NT 1967; entire Bible 1971)

Prepared by Kenneth N. Taylor, a graduate of Northern Baptist Theological Seminary and a former editor at Moody Press, Taylor's *Living Bible, Paraphrased*, has enjoyed the most phenomenal distribution in publishing history. By the mid-1970s, it had captured 46 percent of the total sales of the Bible in the U.S.A. By the close of the century, it had been translated into nearly one hundred languages, together spoken by 90 percent of the world's population, and forty million copies had been printed.

The origin of the rendering was as follows. In order to help his ten children understand the Scriptures during daily family devotions, in 1956 Taylor decided to paraphrase the American Standard Version of 1901 into simple, modern English. He then began to use his forty-five-minute daily train commute between his farm house near Wheaton, Illinois, and Moody Press's Chicago office for this purpose. His work was issued in stages; in 1962 he published the *Living Letters*, in 1965 the *Living Prophecies*, in 1966 the *Living Gospels*, and in 1967 the entire New Testament. In successive stages, by 1971 he had completed the entire Bible, entitled *The Living Bible, Paraphrased*. His paraphrase was so well received that he established his own publishing company, which he named Tyndale House Publishers after William Tyndale, the father of English translations.

In the introduction to *The Living Bible*, Taylor acknowledges that "translations of the Bible by their very nature reveal theological biases. It is wholesome, therefore, to find a paraphrase that is willing to declare itself at the outset." He states that "the theological lodestar in this book has been a rigid evangelical position." The reader will detect the frequent importation of evangelical terms and revivalist clichés into the text, as for example when *righteousness of God* is paraphrased "way to heaven" (Rom. 3:21) or *justification* becomes "glorious life" (Rom. 5:16). References to being "saved" and "lost" are added at various places to the text. The richness of *eternal life* is reduced to "get to heaven" (Mark 10:17), and *gospel* is rendered "wonderful story" (Mark 1:1) or "way to heaven" (Gal. 1:6 [in quotation marks], 11). The Jewish concept of the two ages is obscured or removed, for example, in 1 Corinthians 10:11 and Luke 20:34–35.

Although the language for the most part is clear and easy to understand, unfortunately sometimes the text is expanded at length with imaginative details for which there is no warrant in the original. A clear example is in the opening verse of the Book of Amos. Here the American Standard Version of 1901 gives a literal word-for-word rendering of the Hebrew. It begins, "The words of Amos, who was among the herdsmen of Tekoa. . . ." In *The Living Bible,* this becomes two full sentences: "Amos was a herdsman living in the village of Tekoa. All day long he sat on the hillsides watching the sheep, keeping them from straying." The American Standard Version continues, ". . . which he saw concerning Israel." In *The Living Bible* this becomes: "One day in a vision, God told him some of the things that were going to happen to the nation, Israel. . . . This is his report of what he saw and heard."

On the other hand, besides additions here and there, Taylor's paraphrase has omissions where no textual problem is involved. For example, in Daniel 3:5 and 10, the list of musical instruments is dropped in favor of "when the band strikes up" and "when the band begins to play." In Judges 7:20 the cry "A sword for the Lord" becomes "For the Lord." There are omissions in the New Testament with no textual support for the omission, such as "first" (Luke 12:1) and "that all might believe through him" (John 1:7). "Churches of Christ" (Rom. 16:16) becomes "all the churches here."

The British edition of *The Living Bible, Paraphrased* is purged of Americanisms and adjusted to idioms current in Great Britain. Accordingly, the American "clothes closet" (1 Sam. 21:9) becomes the British "wardrobe," and the chatty "I guess" becomes more primly "I suppose" (1 Sam. 21:4). Instead of the anachronistic euphemism "Saul went into the cave to go to the bathroom" (1 Sam. 24:3), the British edition has "Saul went into a cave to relieve himself" (the Hebrew text says "to cover his feet").

There have also been many other editions of *The Living Bible, Paraphrased* under a variety of titles. These include *The Way* (1972); *The Way: Catholic Version* (1973); *The One-Year Bible* and *The Lindsell Study Bible* (1980); *The Book* (1984); *The Book for Children* (1985); *The Story, from Adam to Armageddon* (1986); *The Alphabetical Bible* (1988; beginning with the Book of Acts and ending with the Book of Zephaniah!); and a *Simplified Living Bible* (1990), which was issued also as *The Bible for Children* and *The Bible for Students.*

More recently Taylor's paraphrastic technique was abandoned in favor of a totally different approach. In 1996 Tyndale House Publishers issued the *Holy Bible, New Living Translation* (NLT). This revision was translated from the original languages using dynamic equivalence rather than paraphrase.

In 1989 the work of preparing the New Living Translation was entrusted to ninety evangelical scholars chosen from various theological backgrounds and denominations (for their names see pages xlvii–l of the introduction). A general reviewer was appointed to oversee work on each of the six major sections of Scripture. Each major section was divided into five smaller sections, each of which was generally assigned to three different scholars who usually had developed expertise in that part of Scripture. Each scholar made a thorough study of the assigned section and submitted a list of proposed revisions to the respective general reviewer, who then evaluated the suggested changes and prepared a first draft. This draft was then further revised by other biblical scholars and by English stylists. Lastly, the Bible Translation Committee reviewed the rendering verse by verse to prepare a final revision.

The rendering of the New Living Translation uses the vocabulary and language structures commonly used by the average person. The result is a translation of the Scriptures aimed generally at the reading level of a junior-high student. The translators were also sensitive to gender-inclusive wording. In the introduction, the reader is informed that

The English language changes constantly. An obvious change is in the area of gender-inclusive language. This creates problems for modern translators of the ancient biblical text, which was originally written in a male-oriented culture. The translator must respect the nature of the ancient context while also accounting for the concerns of the modern audience. Often the original language itself allows a rendering that is gender-inclusive. For example, the Greek word *anthropos*, traditionally rendered "man," really means "human being" or "person." A different Greek word, *aner*, specifically means a male.

There are other occasions where the original language is male-oriented, but not intentionally so. For example, in the Pentateuch most of the laws are stated in language that is replete with masculine pronouns. But since it is clear in many cases that the recipients of these laws were both male and female, we have used gender-neutral language where appropriate. Another example is found in the New Testament epistles, where the believers are called "brothers" (*adelphoi*). Yet it is clear that these epistles were addressed to all the believers—male and female. Thus, we have usually translated this Greek word "brothers and sisters" or "Christian friends" in order to represent the historical situation more accurately.

This feature of gender-neutral language, as well as the generally more dignified and deliberate wording of the translation, can be appreciated when Matthew 7:1–5 is compared with the *Living Bible* paraphrase.

Living Bible	*New Living Translation*
[1]Don't criticize, and then you won't be criticized.	[1]Stop judging others, and you will not be judged.
[2]For others will treat you as you treat them.	[2]For others will treat you as you treat them. Whatever measure you use in judging others, it will be used to measure how you are judged.
[3]And why worry about a speck in the eye of a brother when you have a board in your own?	[3]And why worry about a speck in your friend's eye when you have a log in your own?
[4]Should you say, "Friend, let me help you get that speck out of your eye," when you can't even see because of the board in your own?	[4]How can you think of saying, "Friend, let me help you get rid of that speck in your eye," when you can't see past the log in your own eye?
[5]Hypocrite! First get rid of the board, then you can see to help your brother.	[5]Hypocrite! First get rid of the log from your own eye; then perhaps you will see well enough to deal with the speck in your friend's eye.

Eugene Peterson's *The Message* (NT 1993; OT Wisdom books 1997; OT Prophets 2000)

Eugene H. Peterson's *The Message: The New Testament in Contemporary Language* attempts to do for the 1990s what *The Living Bible* did for the 1970s. Begun while Peterson was serving as pastor of

Christ Our King Presbyterian Church in Bel Air, Maryland, the work was continued after he became professor of spiritual theology at Regent College, Vancouver, Canada.

In the introduction (p. 7), he states the nature of his rendering:

> This version of the New Testament in a contemporary idiom keeps the language of the message current and fresh and understandable in the same language in which we do our shopping, talk with our friends, worry about world affairs, and teach our children their table manners. The goal is not to render a word-for-word conversion of Greek into English, but rather to convert the tone, the rhythm, the events, the ideas, into the way we actually think and speak.

While Peterson attempts to produce an informal rendering, his primary interest is not to choose simple English words (in fact, he uses such words as "addendum," "chagrined," "consummate," "curt," "embryonic," "perigee," and "resplendent"), but words that forcefully convey the meaning to the reader. At the same time, he goes beyond the acceptable bounds of dynamic equivalence in that he will often divest passages from their first-century Jewish context, so that Jesus, for example, sounds like a twentieth-century American. In Matthew 5:41–42, Jesus says, "If someone takes unfair advantage of you, use the occasion to practice the servant life. No more tit-for-tat stuff. Live generously." No longer are we in first-century Judea, where Roman occupation troops had the right to require Jews to carry their packs.

Besides indulging in transculturation, at times Peterson pads the text with additional details in the interest of heightening the vividness and drama. Colossians 1:20 reads: "Not only that, but all the broken and dislocated pieces of the universe—people and things, animals and atoms—get properly fixed and fit together in vibrant harmonies, all because of his death, his blood that poured down from the Cross."

John's version of the heavenly Christ (Rev. 1:12–16) is presented as follows:

> I saw a gold menorah
>   with seven branches,
> And in the center, the Son of Man,
>   in a robe and gold breastplate,
>   hair in a blizzard of white,

> Eyes pouring fire-blaze,
>   both feet furnace-fired bronze,
> His voice a cataract,
>   right hand holding seven stars,
> His mouth a sharp-biting sword,
>   his face a perigee sun.

Paul's enumeration of the desires of the flesh (Gal. 5:19–21) turns out as follows:

It is obvious what kind of life develops out of trying to get your own way all the time: repetitive, loveless, cheap sex; a stinking accumulation of mental and emotional garbage; frenzied and joyless grabs for happiness; trinket gods; magic-show religion; paranoid loneliness; cutthroat competition; all-consuming-yet-never-satisfied wants; a brutal temper; an impotence to love or be loved; divided homes and divided lives; small-minded and lopsided pursuits; the vicious habit of depersonalizing everyone into a rival; uncontrolled and uncontrollable addictions; ugly parodies of community. I could go on.

Finally, the simple language of Jesus concerning prayer recorded in the Sermon on the Mount (Matt. 6:7–13) is transmogrified as follows:

The world is full of so-called prayer warriors who are prayer-ignorant. They're full of formulas and programs and advice, peddling techniques for getting what you want from God. Don't fall for that nonsense. This is your Father you are dealing with, and he knows better than you what you need. With a God like this loving you, you can pray very simply. Like this:

> Our Father in heaven,
> Reveal who you are.
> Set the world right;
> Do what's best—
>   as above, so below.
> Keep us alive with three square meals.
> Keep us forgiven with you and forgiving others.
> Keep us safe from ourselves and the Devil.
> You're in charge!
> You can do anything you want!
> You're ablaze in beauty!
>   Yes. Yes. Yes.

Peterson has begun to issue books of the Old Testament as part of *The Message*. Thus far, Psalms, Proverbs, Job, Ecclesiastes, and the Song of Songs have been published (1997), as well as the Prophets (2000).[5]

---

5. They are available from NavPress, P.O. Box 35001, Colorado Springs, CO 80935.

Postscript

The first translation of the whole Bible into English is commonly attributed to John Wycliffe, an eminent Oxford theologian of the fourteenth century (c. 1330–84). From that time to the close of the twentieth century, translators have produced a wide variety of English versions of the Bible and of the New Testament. The list published by Alan S. Duthie in 1995 contains "nearly sixty more or less different English versions of the whole Bible; plus another seventy-five of the New Testament."[1] Another list was drawn up by Laurence M. Vance in "an attempt to comprehensively tabulate all English translations of the Bible since 1611 [embracing] complete Bibles or separate Old or New Testaments."[2] From the King James Bible of 1611 until 1991, Vance records a total of 291 translations. In both reckonings, it was during the twentieth century that a proliferation of translations took place.

An obvious reason why English versions differ from one another is the slow, ongoing modification of the English language. Another is the adoption of a particular style and level of English diction suited to a particular age-group or reading public. Beyond such considerations, however, versions of the Bible differ from one another because of several kinds of basic problems—textual, lexical, literary, and grammatical—that confront all translators.

1. Alan S. Duthie, *How to Choose Your Bible Wisely*, 2d ed. (Carlisle, U.K.: Paternoster, 1995), p. 13.

2. Laurence M. Vance, *A Brief History of English Bible Translations* (Pensacola, Fla.: Vance Publications, 1993), p. 103.

Differences of Wording among Manuscripts

The first problem confronting translators is the presence of differences of wording among manuscripts of the Scriptures. These differences have arisen because a scribe in copying a document of some considerable length would, almost inevitably, make inadvertent alterations in the wording. Furthermore, occasionally a scribe would deliberately introduce into the copy a slight change that seemed to be needed in order to clarify the meaning. For example, the older manuscripts of Mark 1:2–3 attribute to the prophet Isaiah the Evangelist's quotations from both Malachi and Isaiah, whereas later manuscripts (followed by the King James translators of 1611) read, "as it is written in the prophets"—an obvious amelioration of the earlier text.

Versions of the Bible differ because translators have differed in deciding which variant readings should be preferred as original and which are secondary. In general, the wording of older manuscripts can be trusted as likely to have suffered fewer scribal alterations than recent manuscripts, since the latter are probably descendants of repeated stages of copying and recopying. It is noteworthy that on the basis of one of the ancient Dead Sea Scrolls, the NRSV has added four sentences at the close of 1 Samuel 10.

For obvious reasons, the variant reading that makes a clarification of a difficulty in the text is generally regarded as a secondary reading. If, however, such a reading has had wide circulation in the manuscripts, the translator may decide that it deserves to be made available in a footnote, introduced by the statement "Other ancient authorities read. . . ."

The Meaning of Words

After the translator has decided which form of the Hebrew or Greek text should be taken as the basis of the new rendering, the next problem has to do with ascertaining the meaning of the words. The Hebrew Scriptures contain several hundred words that have not been found in any other literature and are therefore difficult to translate. One such word is *pim,* which occurs only in 1 Samuel 13:21. This word was taken by the translators of the King James Version to mean "a file," used by blacksmiths to sharpen hoes and other agricultural tools. During the twentieth century, however, archaeologists discovered at various places in Palestine ancient sets of weights used for business transactions, each bearing a Hebrew word. One of these is marked *pim*—consequently, translators now know that this is the amount the blacksmith charged for sharpening various tools.

The Greek New Testament contains relatively few rare words (no more than two dozen) that occur in no other literature. One of them, however, is an important word in the Lord's Prayer (Matt. 6:11; Luke 11:3). In the petition for God to give us "our *epiousion* bread," the adjective has been analyzed by lexicographers to mean either "daily" bread or bread "for tomorrow." When a Hebrew or Greek word may legitimately be taken in two different ways, the translator usually provides both renderings, placing one in the text and the other in a footnote. The latter will be introduced by the word "Or."

Adding Modern Punctuation

Once the translator has decided which wording of the text to translate and what the Hebrew or Greek words mean, the problem of punctuation arises. In antiquity, scribes wrote Hebrew and Greek manuscripts with few, if any, marks of punctuation. Modern editors of the texts and translators must therefore decide where a new sentence begins and where to insert commas, question marks, quotation marks, and other punctuation. Naturally, opinions will sometimes differ. For example, the Lord's Prayer in the King James Bible reads, "Thy will be done in earth, as it is in heaven" (Matt. 6:10), whereas most modern versions punctuate it differently, "Your will be done, on earth as it is in heaven." The principle that translators follow is to insert the punctuation that gives the best and fullest sense. In this case, the second way of punctuating is better, for it permits the phrase "on earth as it is in heaven" to be taken with all three of the preceding petitions ("Hallowed be thy name [on earth as it is in heaven], thy kingdom come [on earth as it is in heaven], thy will be done, on earth as it is in heaven").

Grammatical Problems

A variety of problems arise in the broad category of grammar. One problem is deciding when a given Hebrew or Greek word should be rendered by an English equivalent (translated) and when it should simply be presented in English letters (transliterated). In the Book of Genesis, for example, when should *ʾadam* be translated "man," and when should it be transliterated as a proper name (Adam)? In this matter, ancient and modern translators have varied widely in their judgment. The first use of "Adam" in Targum Pseudo-Jonathan is at Genesis 2:7; in the Greek Septuagint, at 2:16; in the Latin Vulgate, at 2:19; in the NIV, at 2:21; in the NEB, at 3:21; and in the NRSV, at 5:1. The Greek word *Christos* may by transliterated "Christ" or translated "anointed [one]" (i.e., "Messiah"). The Greek verb *baptizō* may be transliterated "baptize" or translated "immerse." The Greek adjective *presbyteros* may be transliterated "presbyter" or translated "elder."

During the past several years, yet another problem has begun to confront translators of the English Bible—the question of the suitability of continuing to use masculine-oriented language in passages that apply to both sexes. Particularly problematic is the question of how one can compensate for the absence in English of a common gender third-person singular pronoun referring to persons. In Matthew 18:2, the King James Version reads "Jesus called a little child unto him, and set him in the midst of them." But since the Greek word *paidion* does not indicate whether the child was a boy or a girl, the translator should hesitate to use either personal pronoun, "him" or "her." Here the NRSV resolves the difficulty by rendering "whom he put among them."

Finally, it must be acknowledged that no translation of the Scriptures is perfect, as anyone who has tried to make one will readily agree. In fact, such features as plays on words (e.g., Jer. 1:11–12; Matt. 16:18; and the deuterocanonical book Susanna 54–55, 58–59) or the alphabetic acrostics (e.g., Ps. 37; Lam. 1, 2, 4) defy the ingenuity of the translator. Ordinarily, along with a translation, no more than a description and/or transliteration of the textual features can be given in a footnote.

Despite all of the difficulties mentioned above, readers of the several translations described in this volume ought to consider what the translators of the King James Bible declared in their statement to the reader: "We affirm and avow, that the very meanest [in modern English = 'worst'] translation of the Bible in *English* . . . containeth the word of God, nay, is the word of God: as the King's speech which he uttered in Parliament, being translated into *French, Dutch, Italian,* and *Latin,* is still the King's speech, though it be not interpreted by every translator with the like grace, nor peradventure so fitly for phrase, nor so expressly for sense, every where."[3]

---

3. Erroll F. Rhodes and Liana Lupas, eds., *The Translators to the Reader: The Original Preface of the King James Version of 1611 Revisited* (New York: American Bible Society, 1997), p. 47, italics in original.

Subject Index

Scripture Index